MW00872970

FASHION
COLORING BOOK
FOR GIRLS

Thank you for choosing NALREZ Publishing.

Copyright © 2022 by NALREZ Publishing
All rights reserved

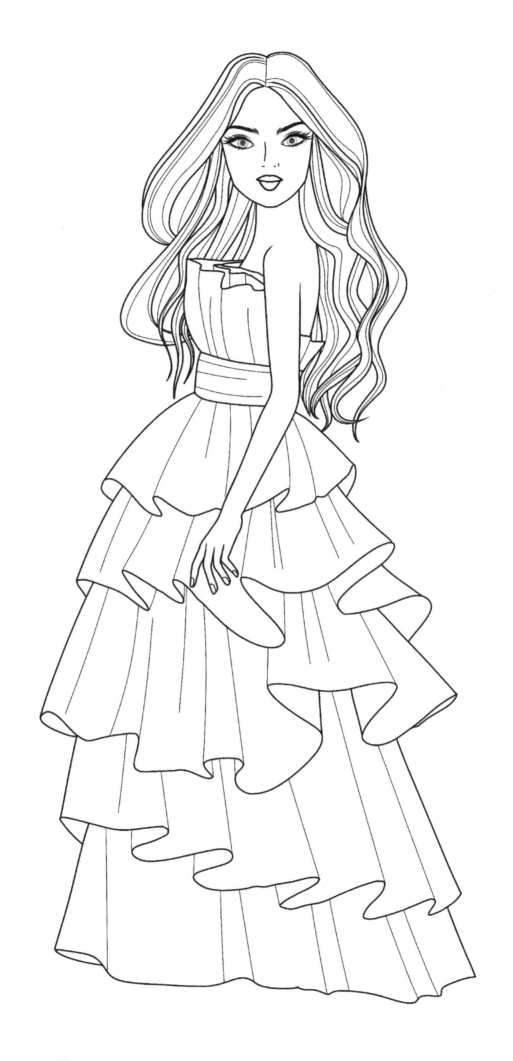

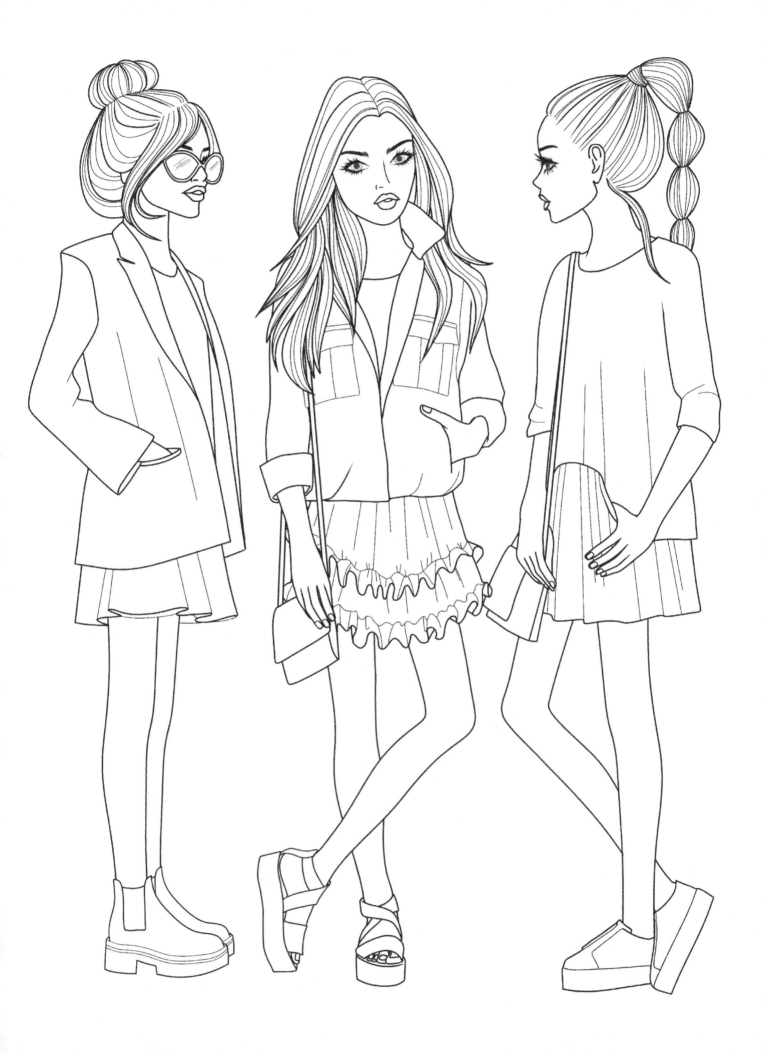

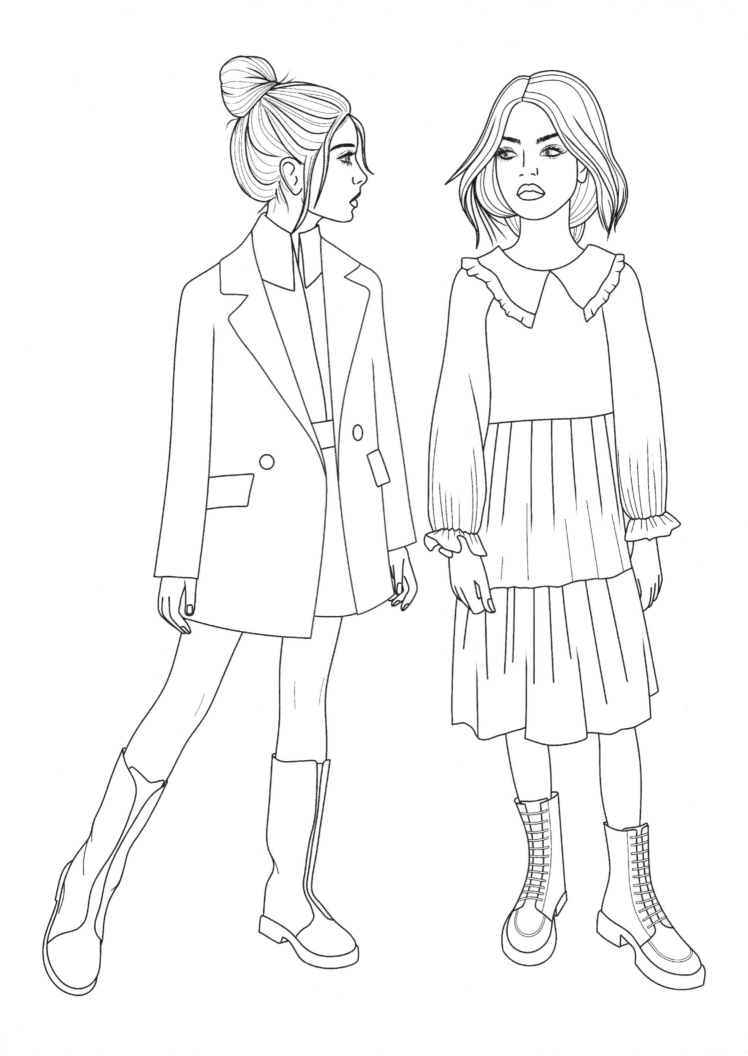

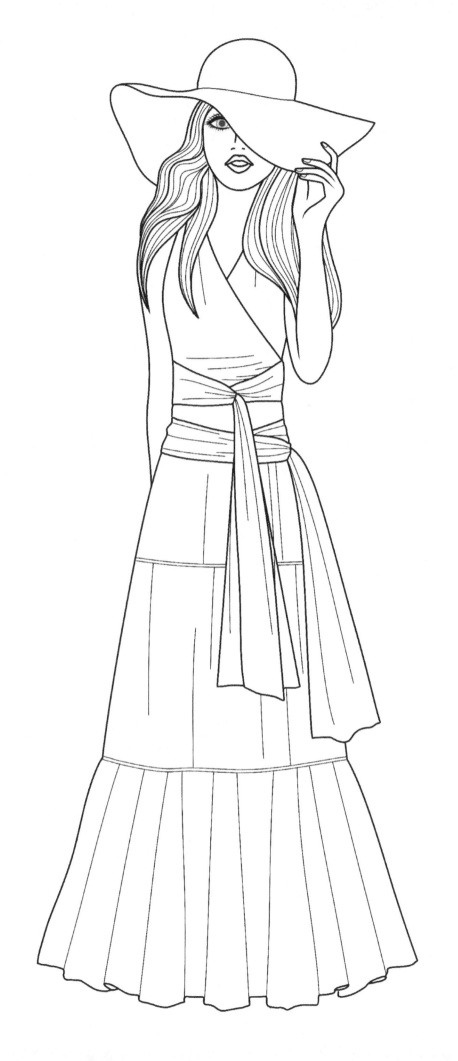

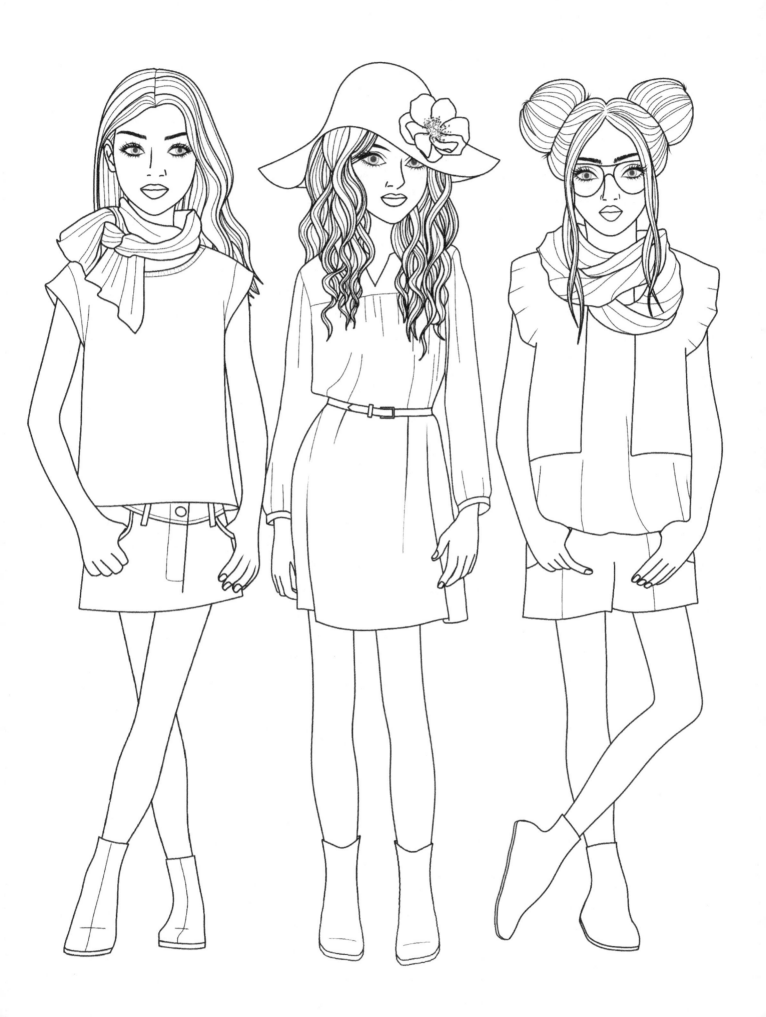

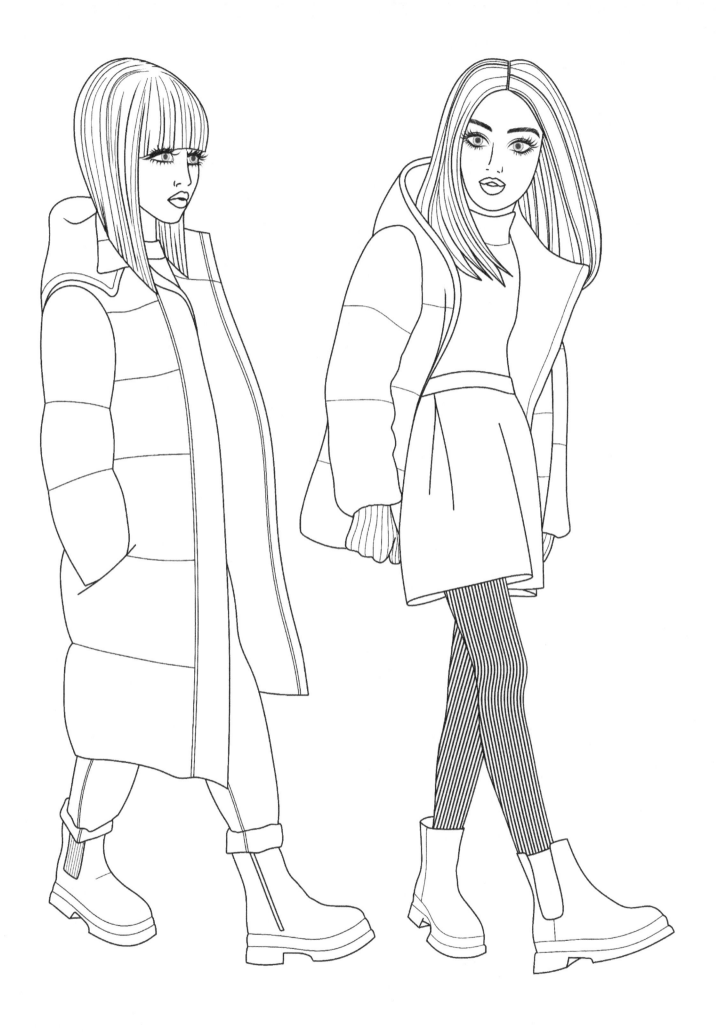

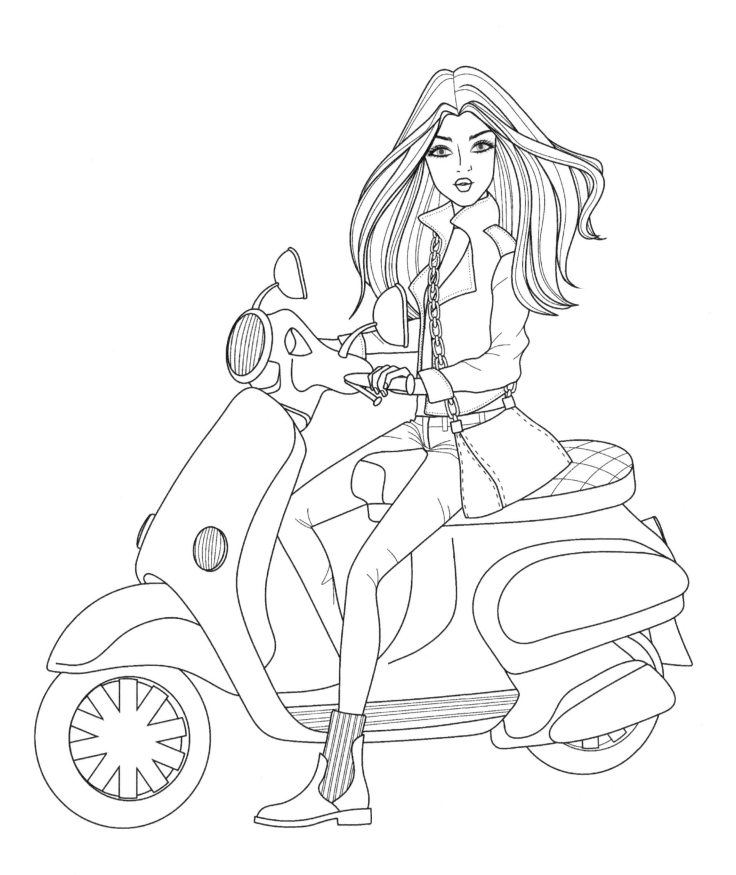

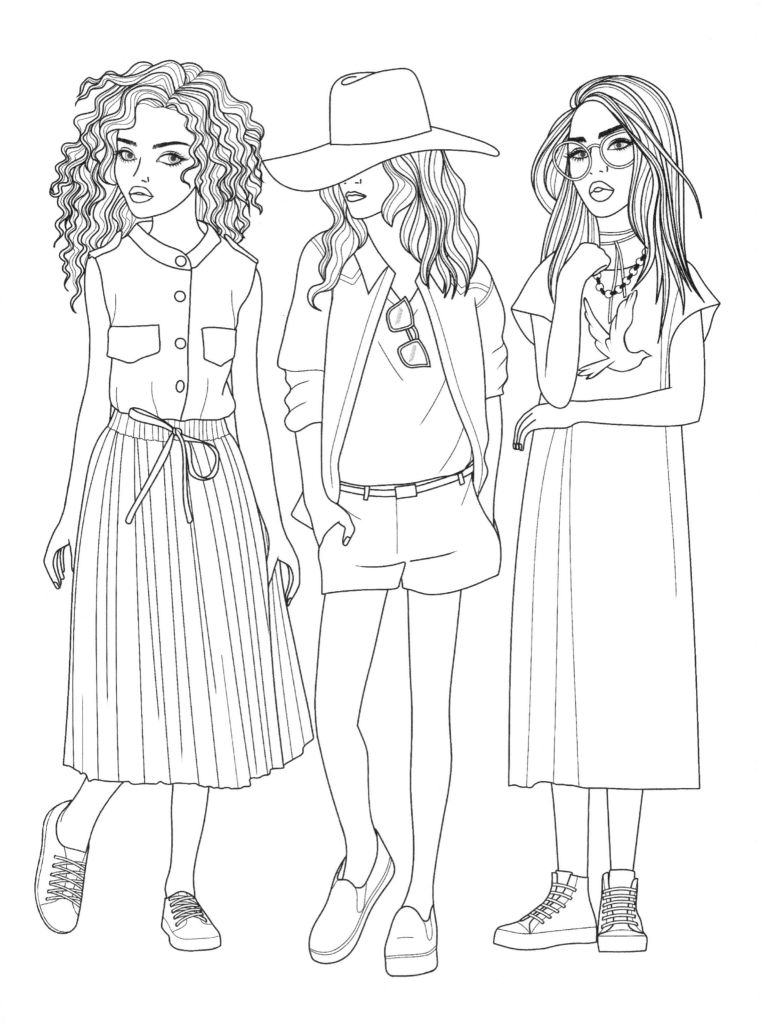

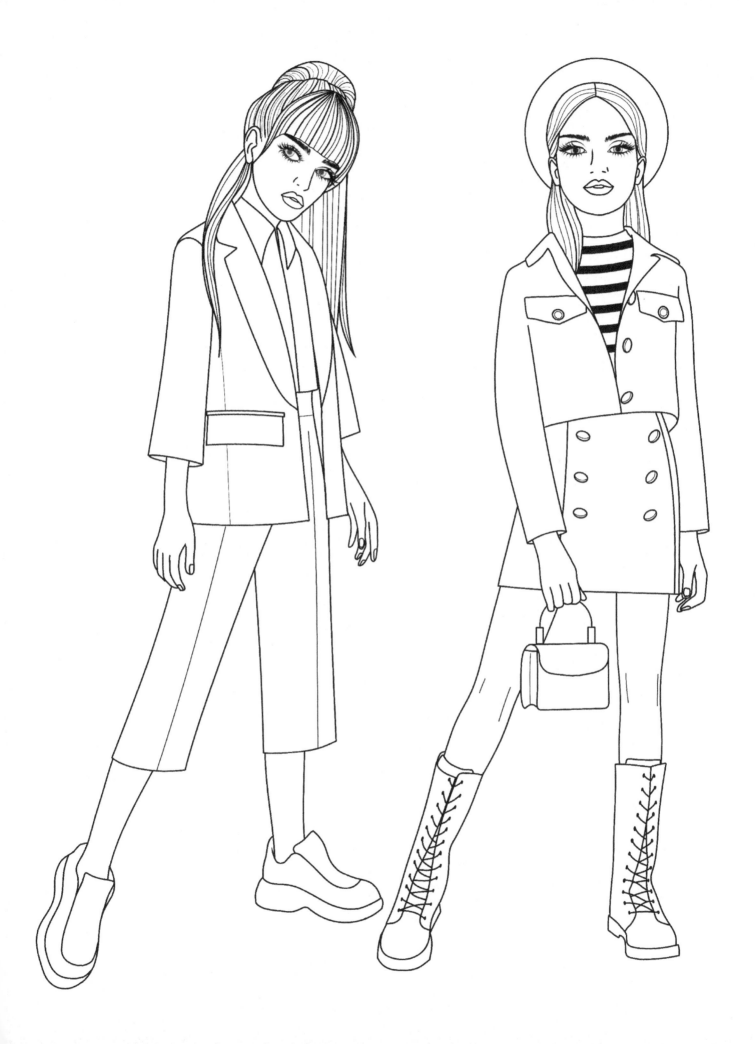

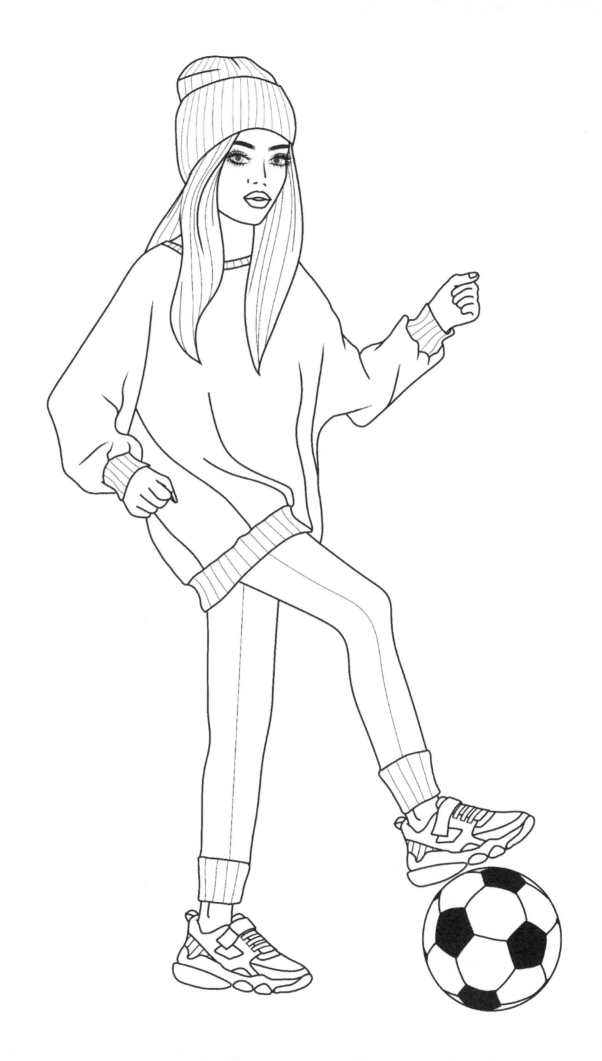

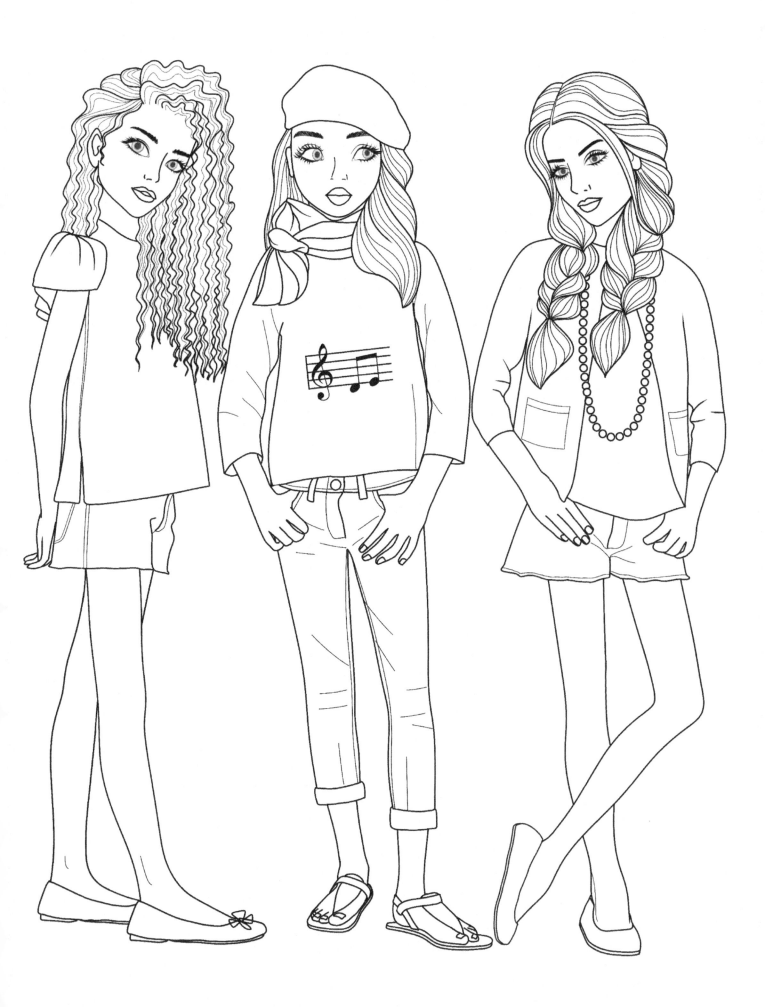

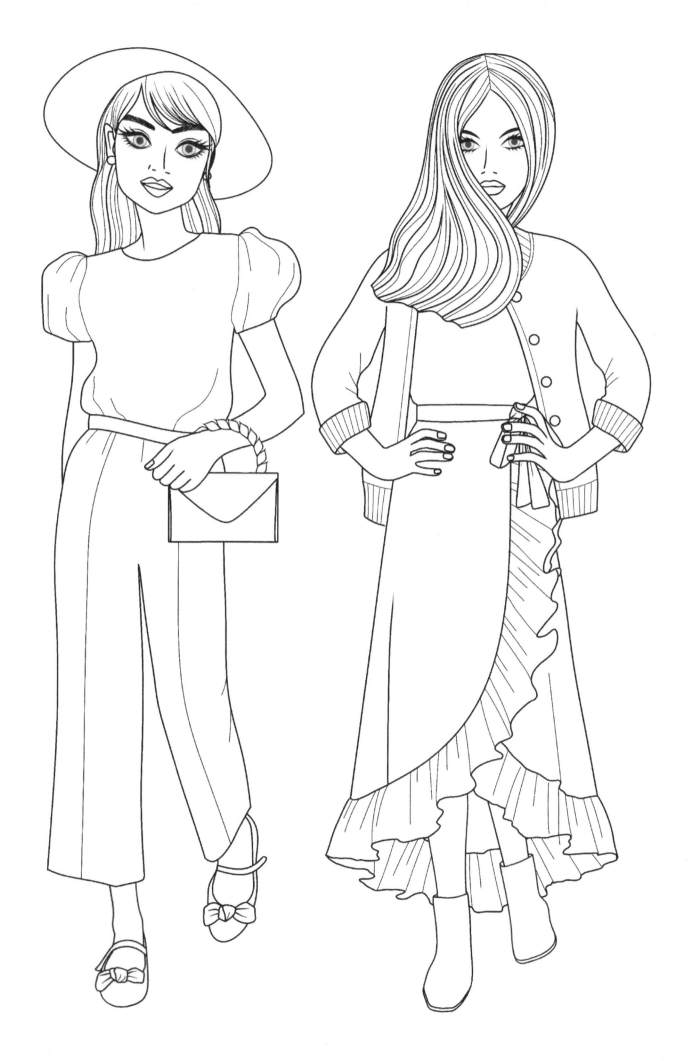

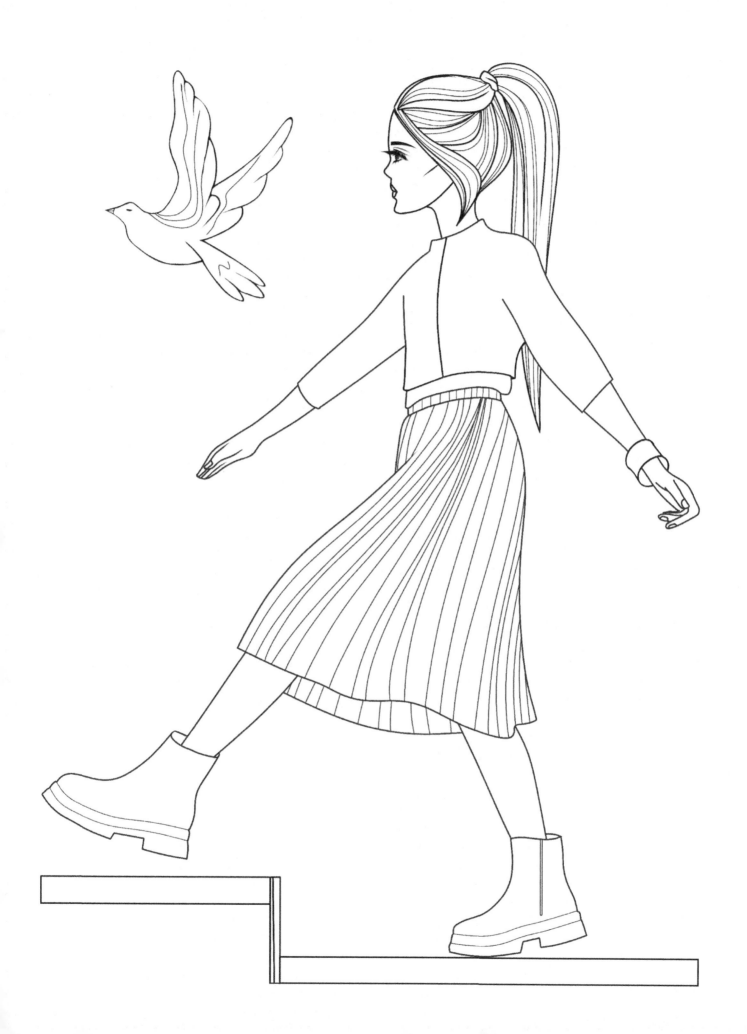

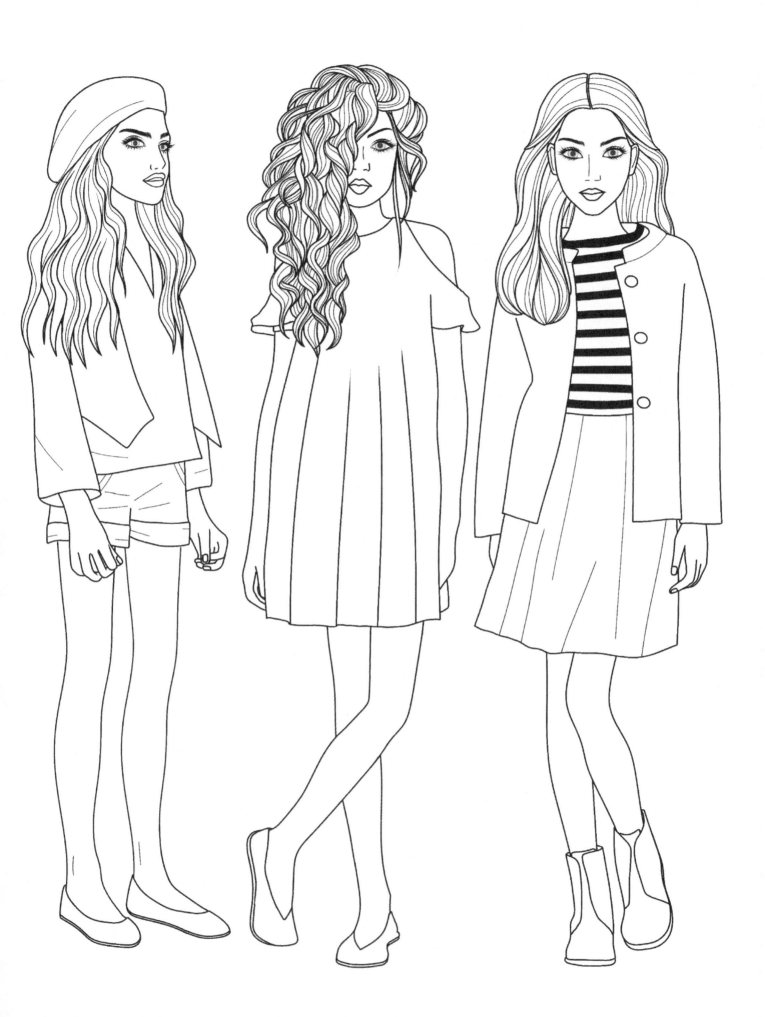

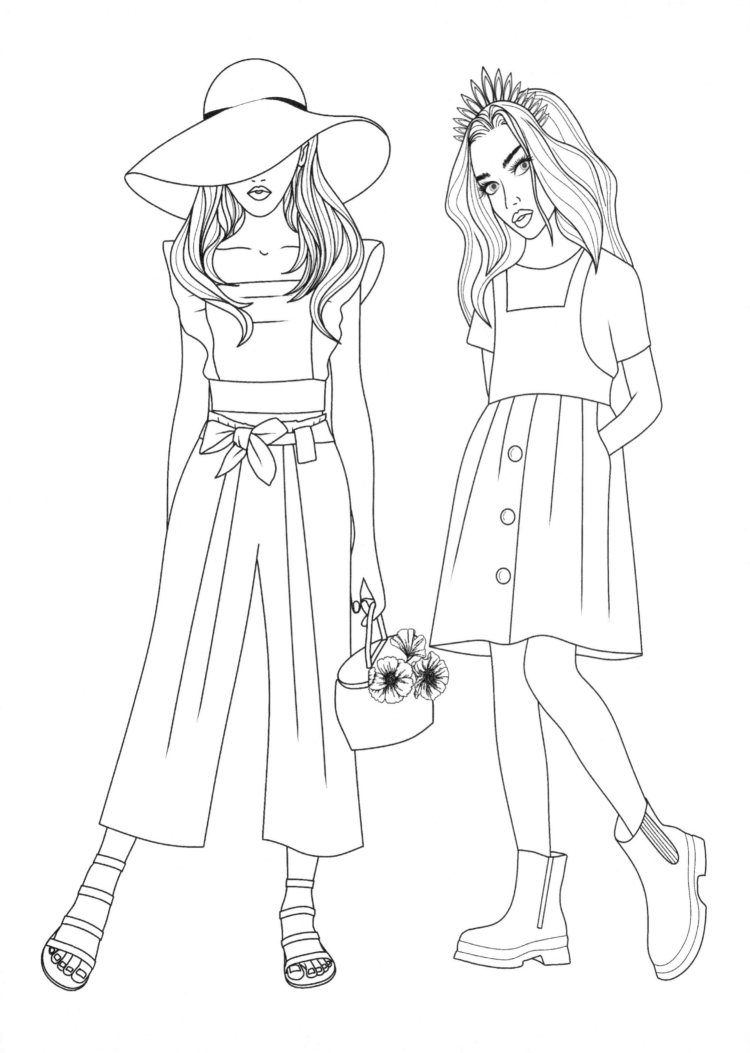

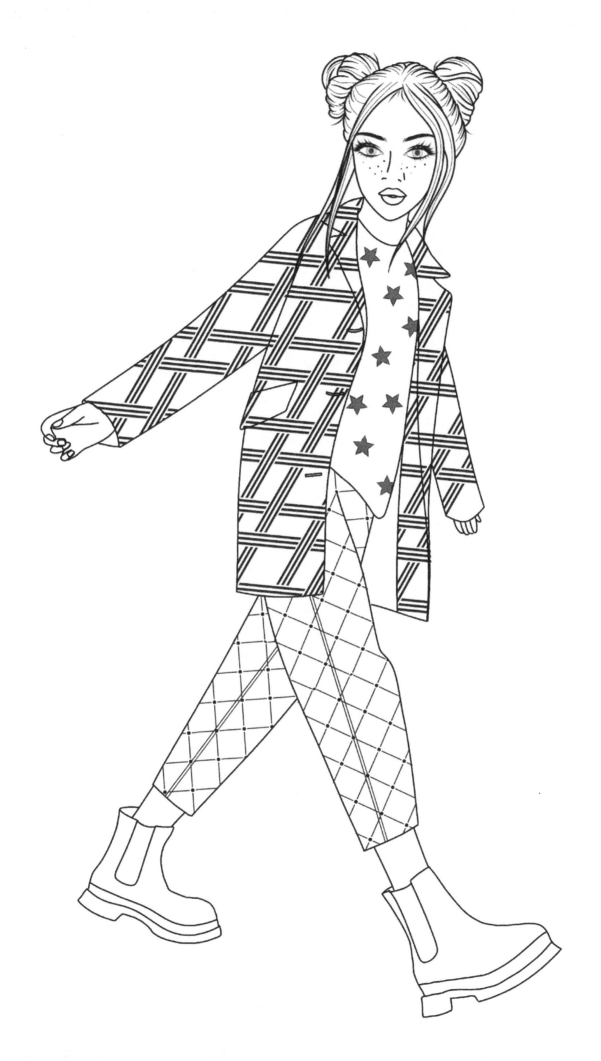

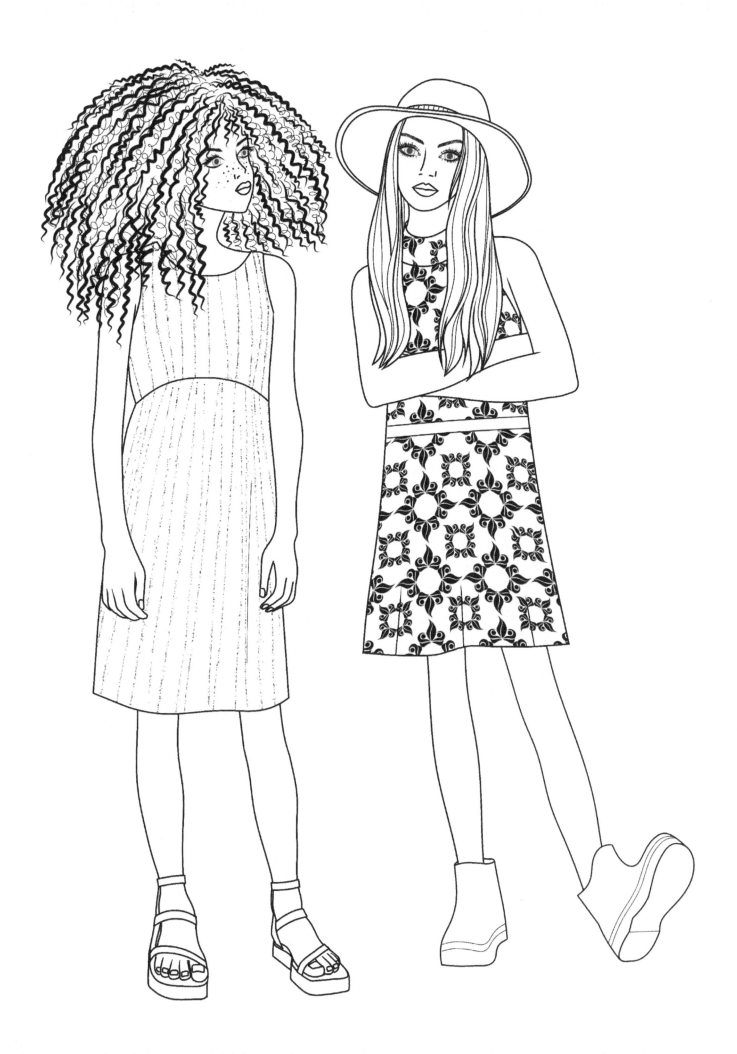

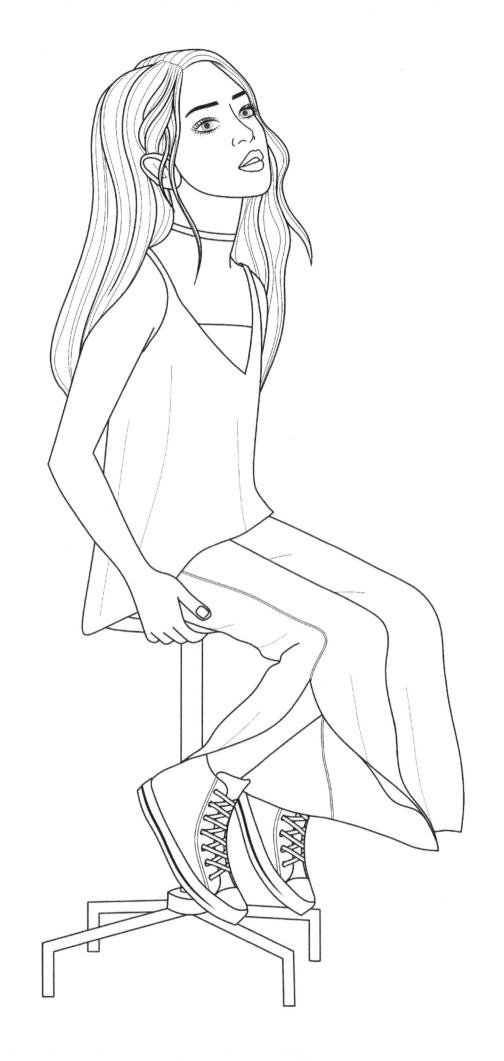

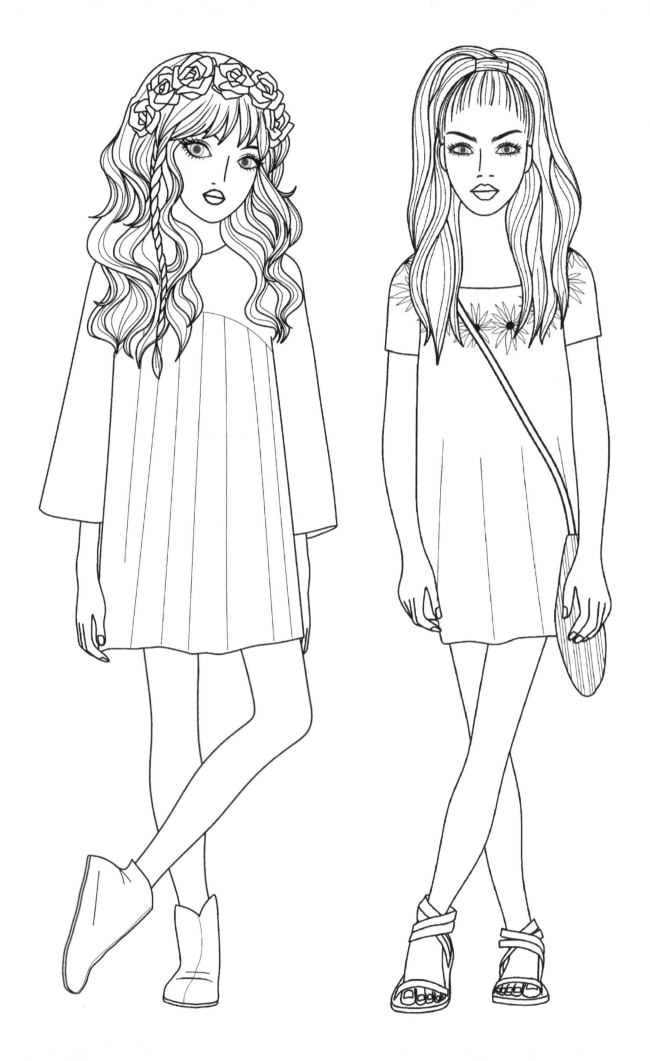

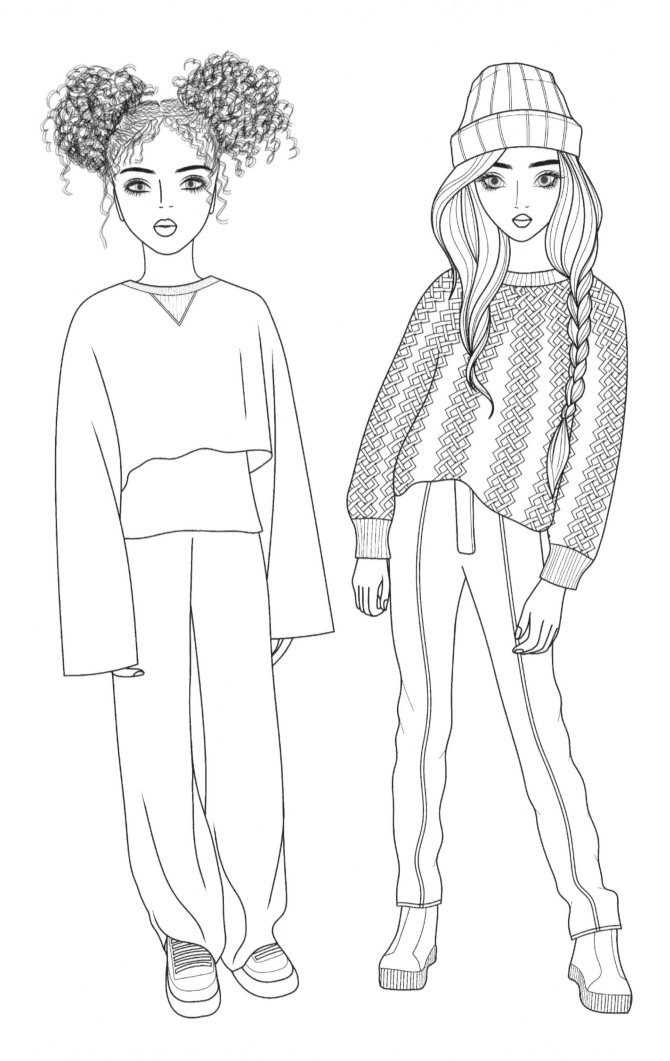

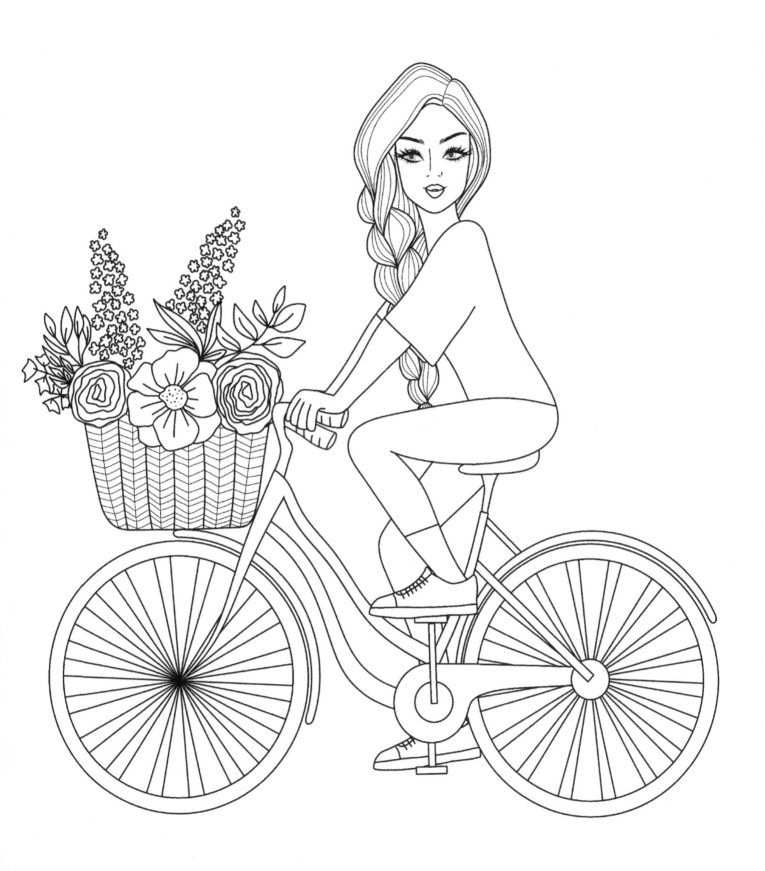

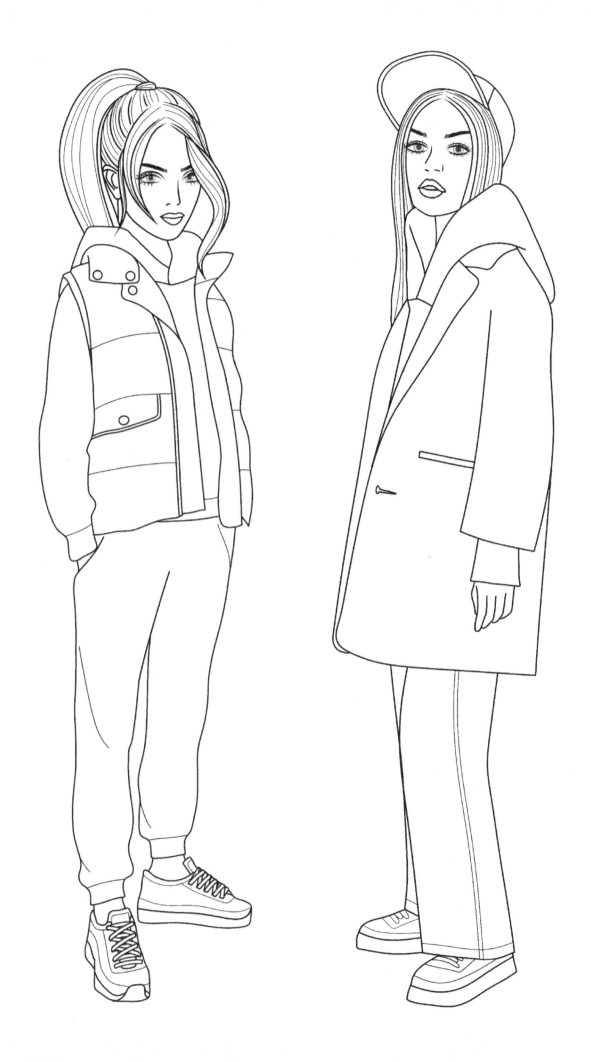

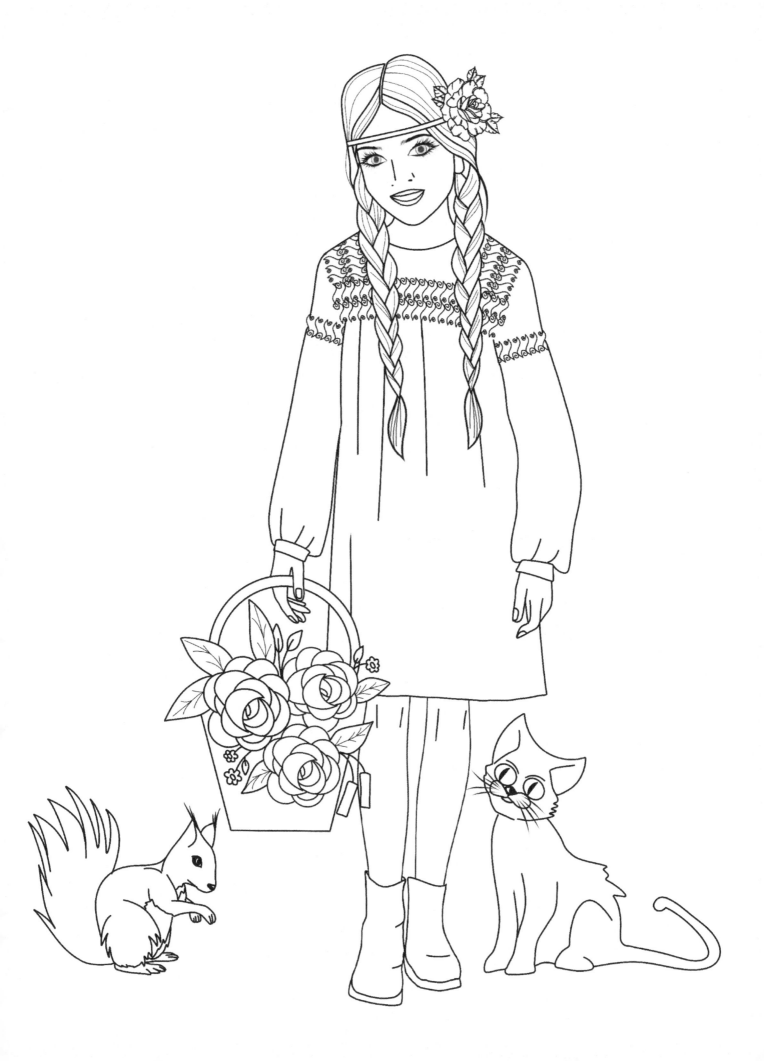

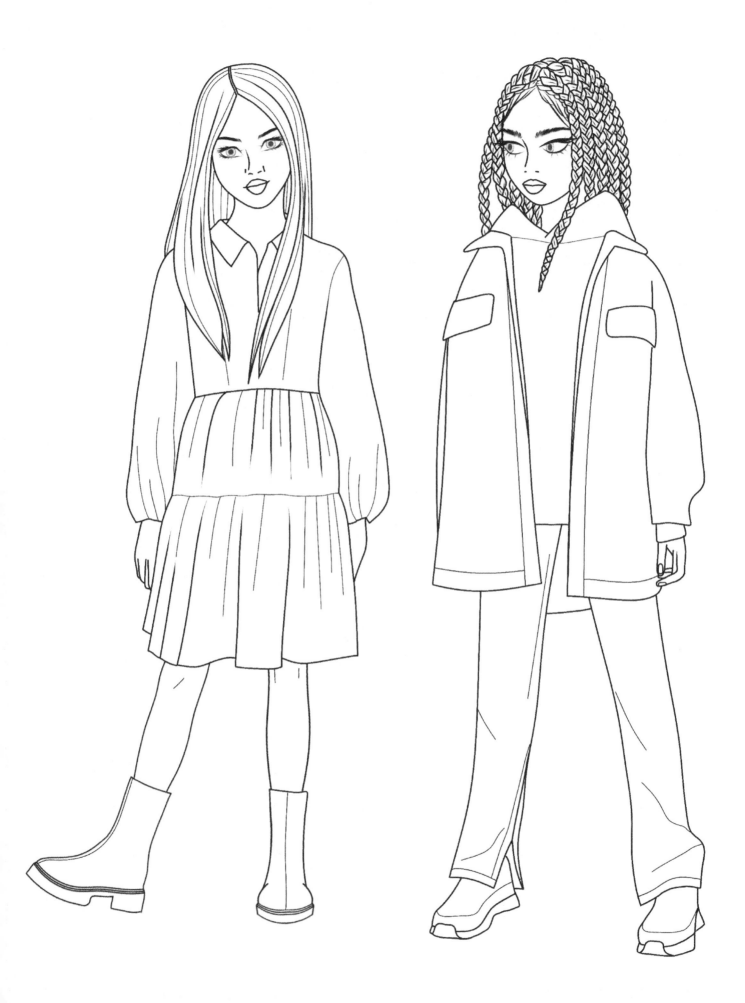

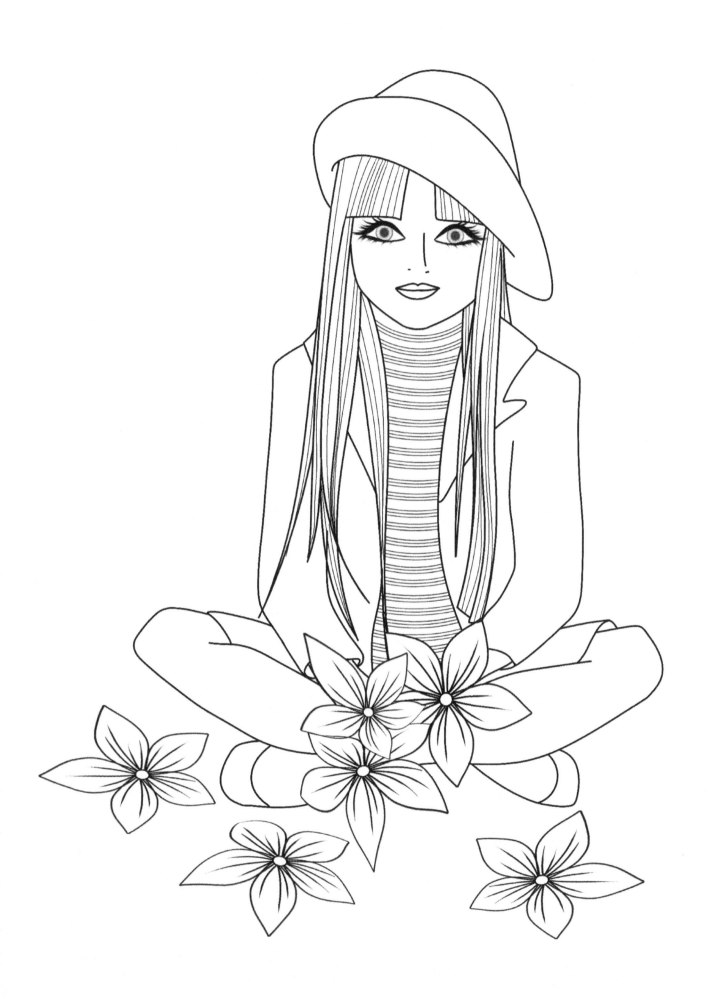

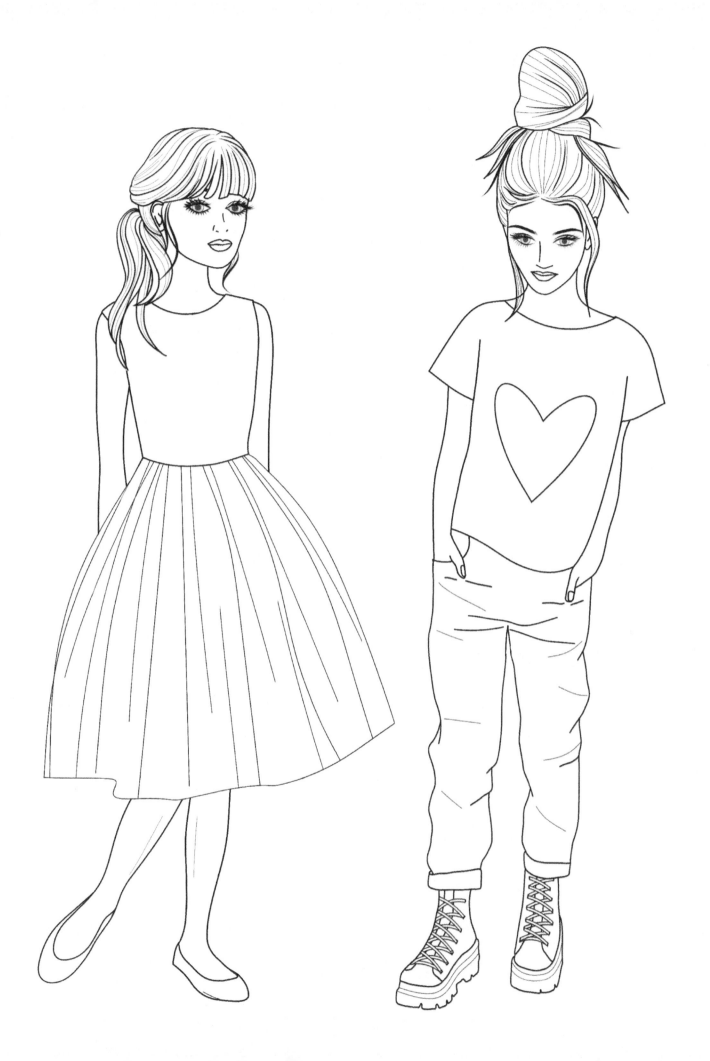

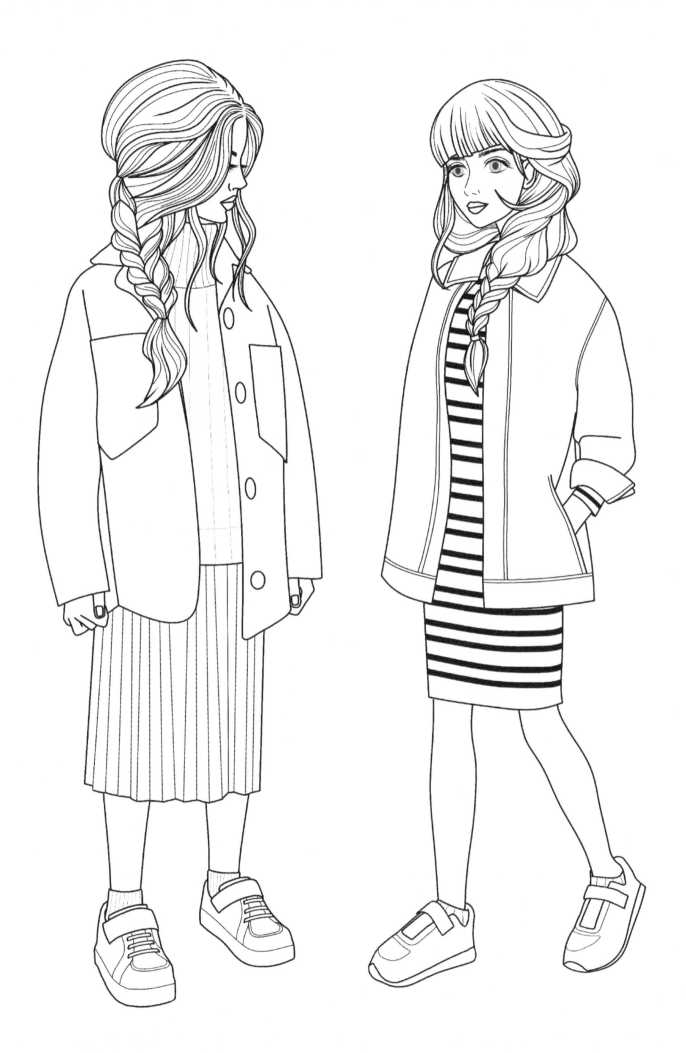

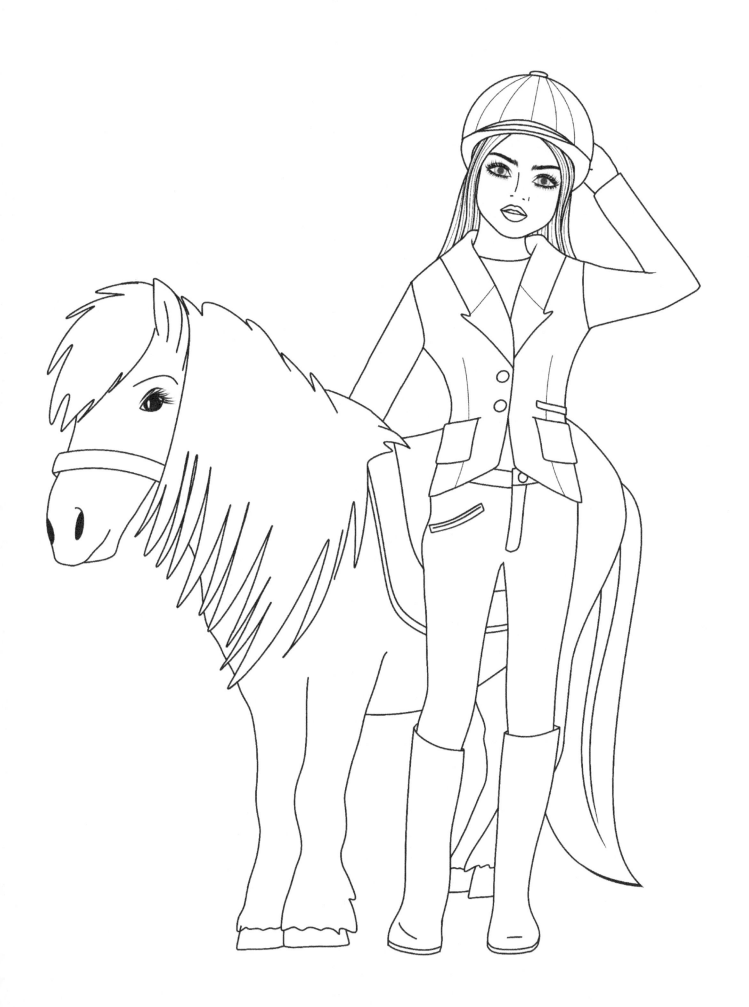

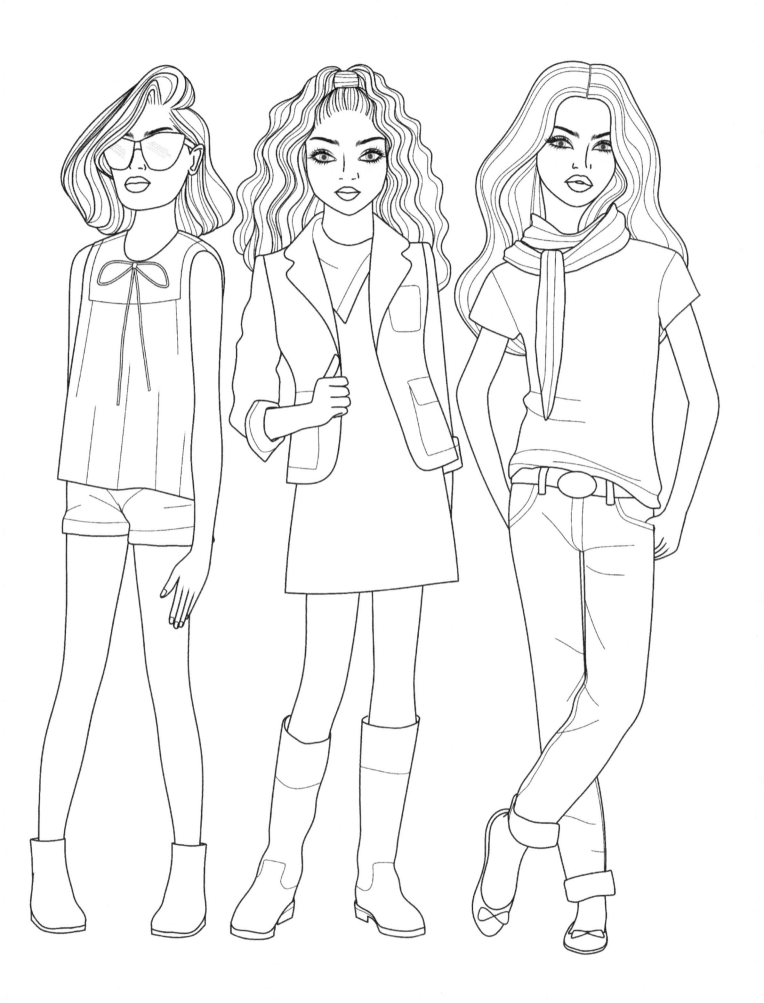

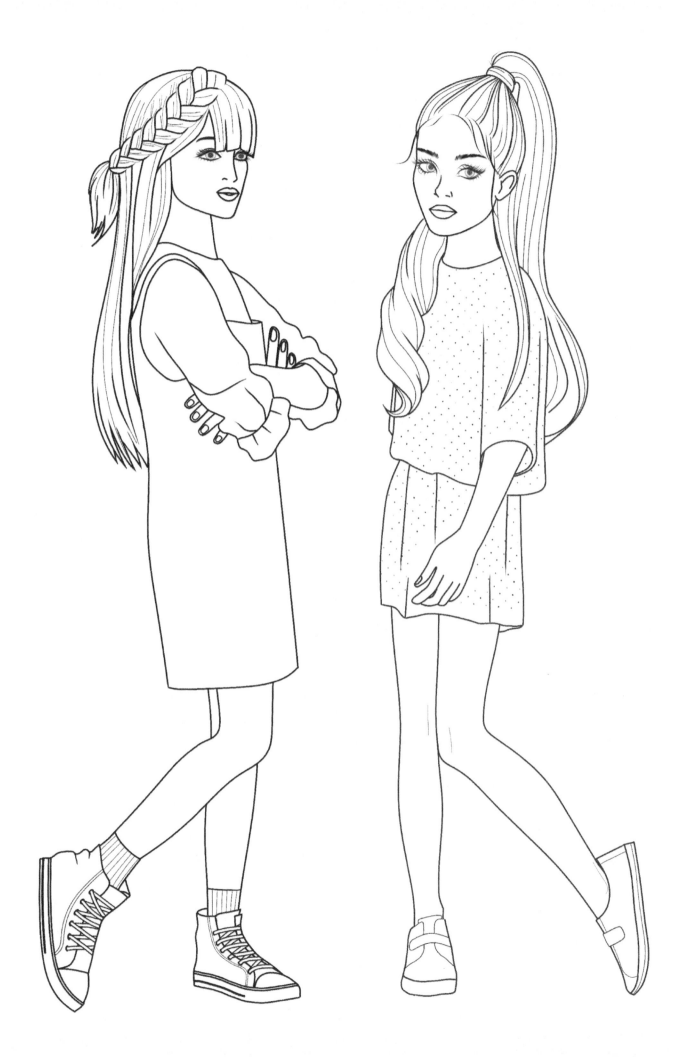

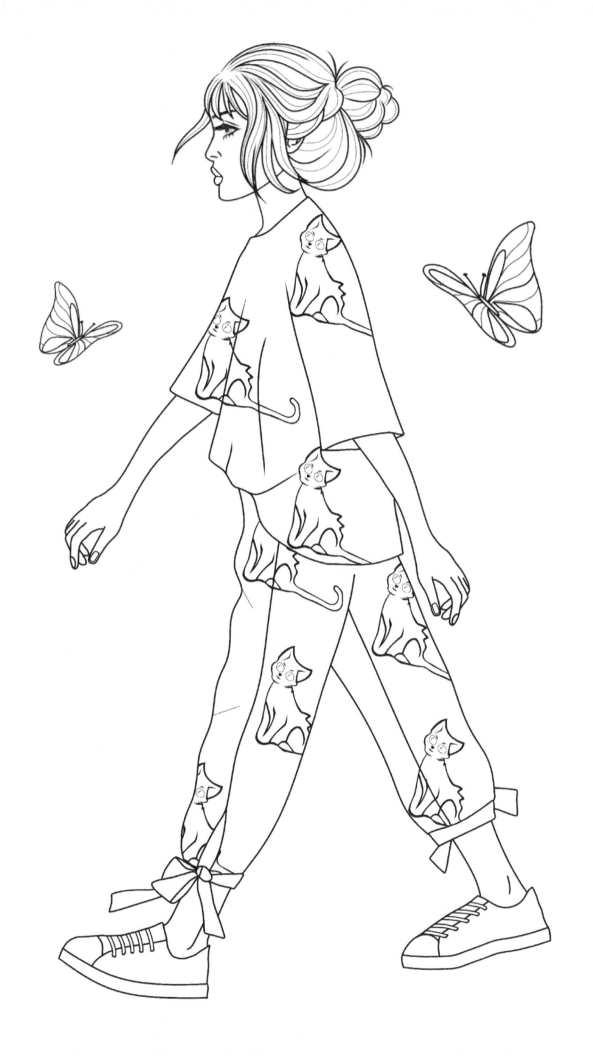

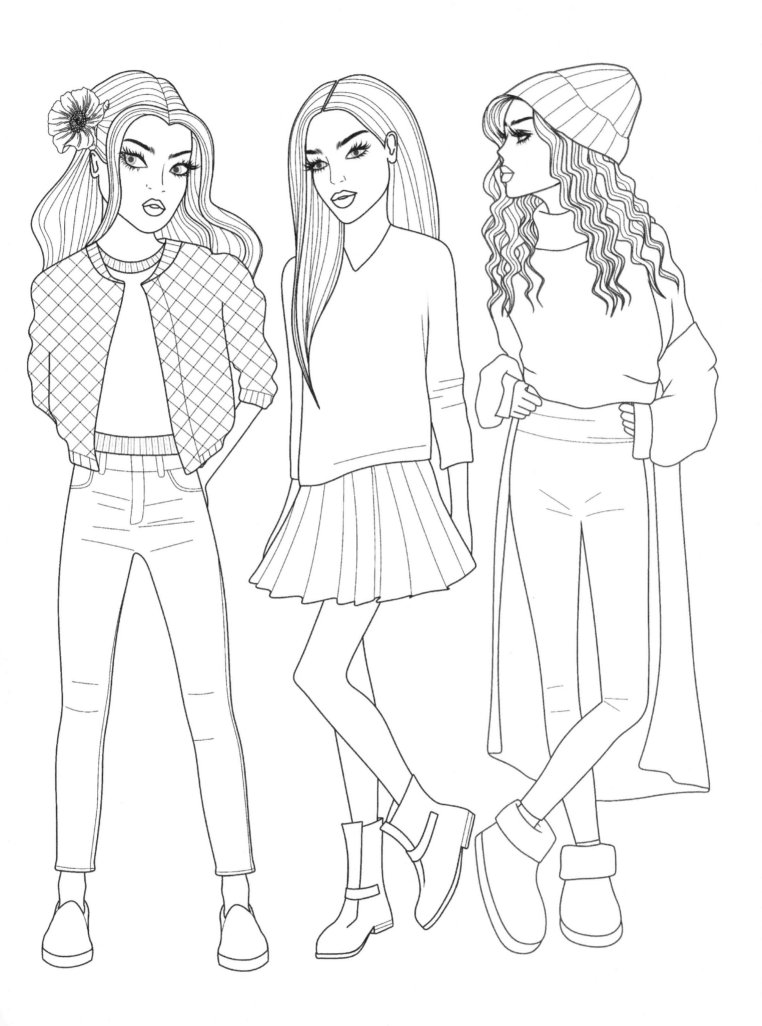

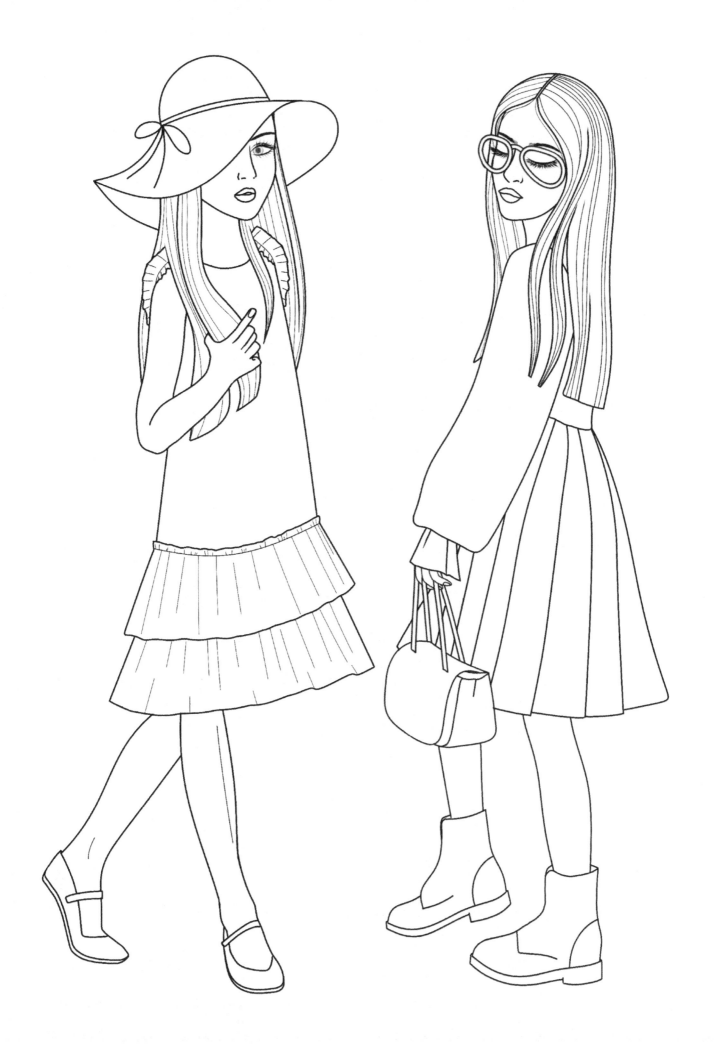

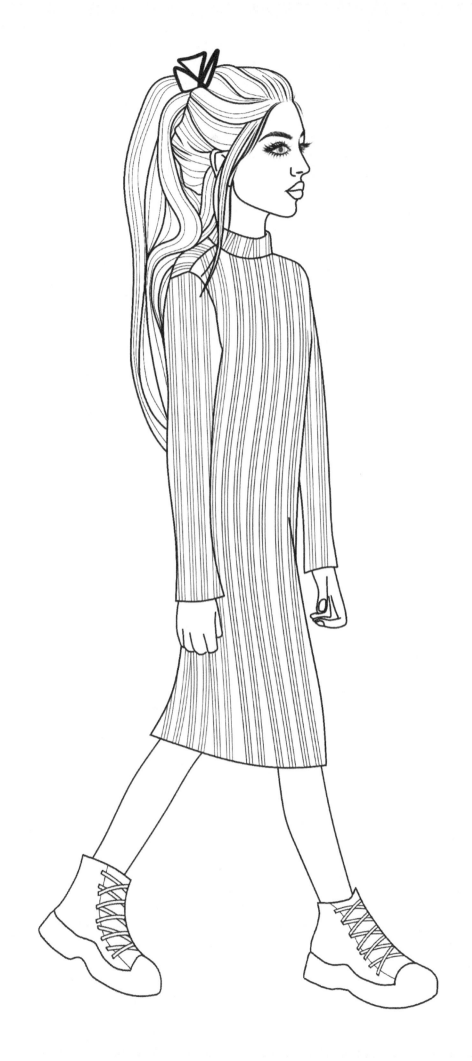

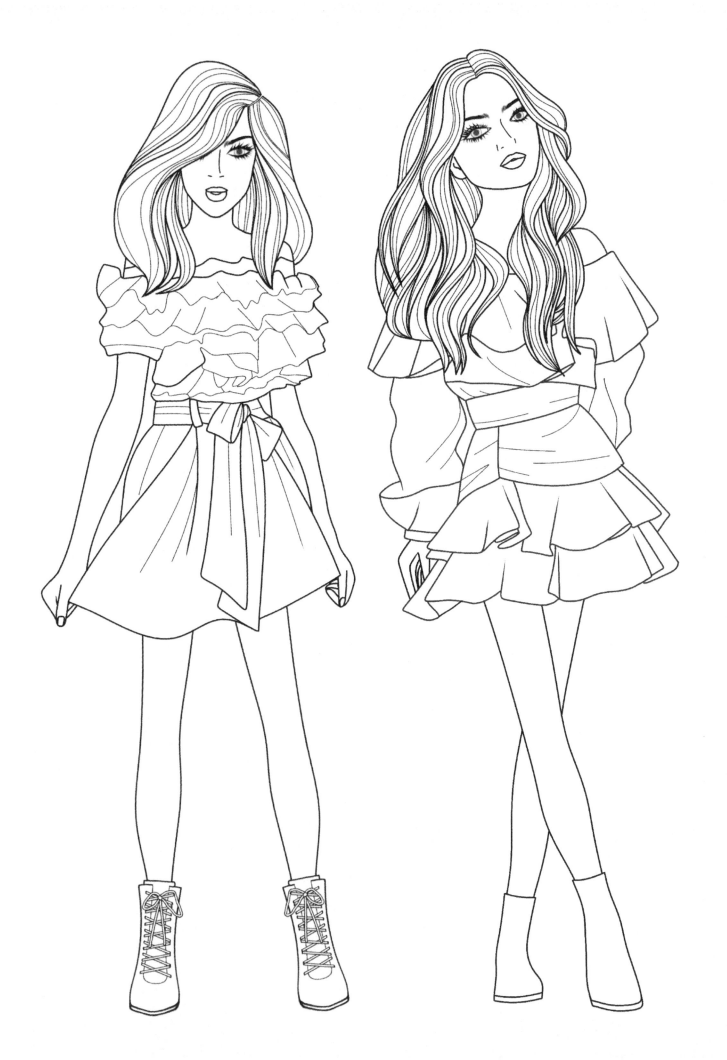

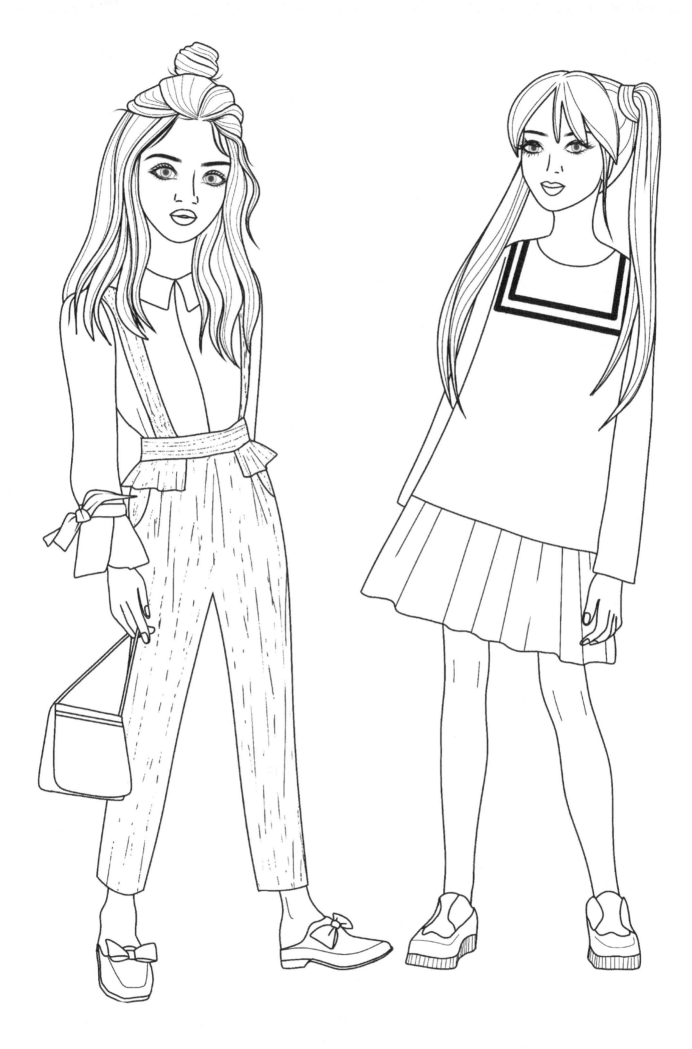

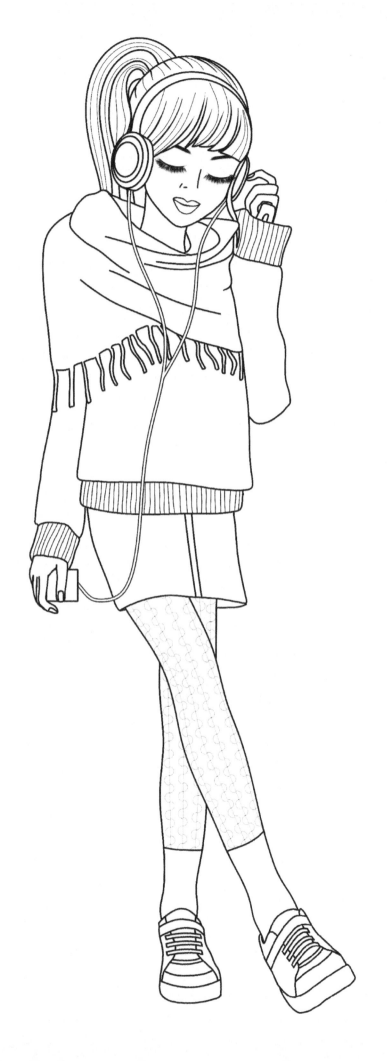

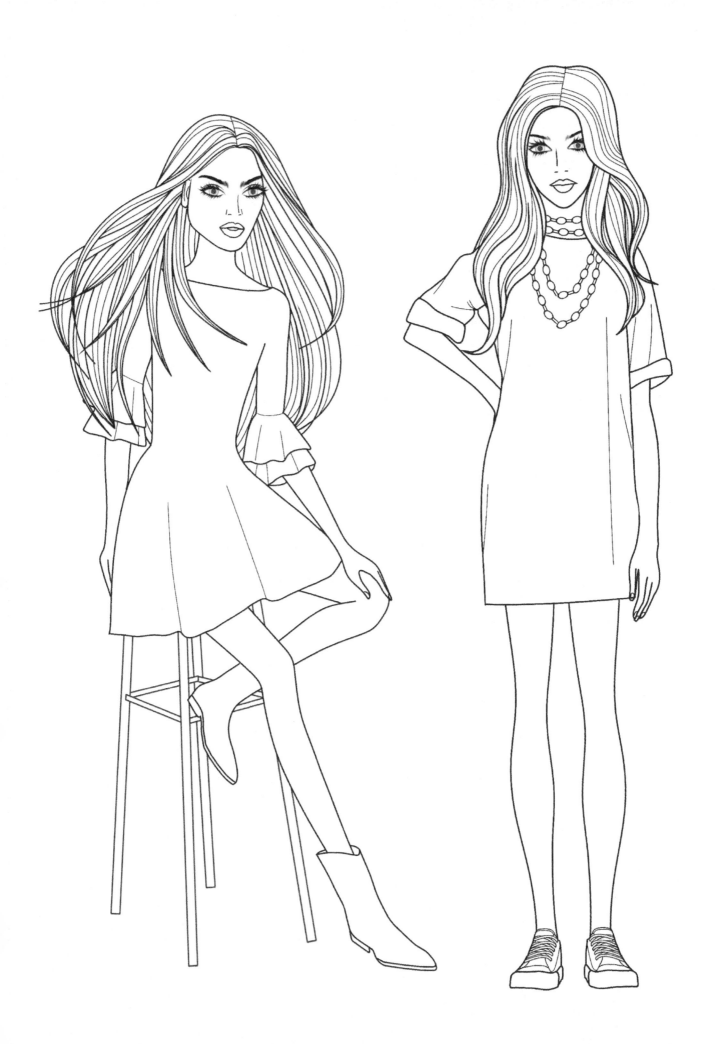

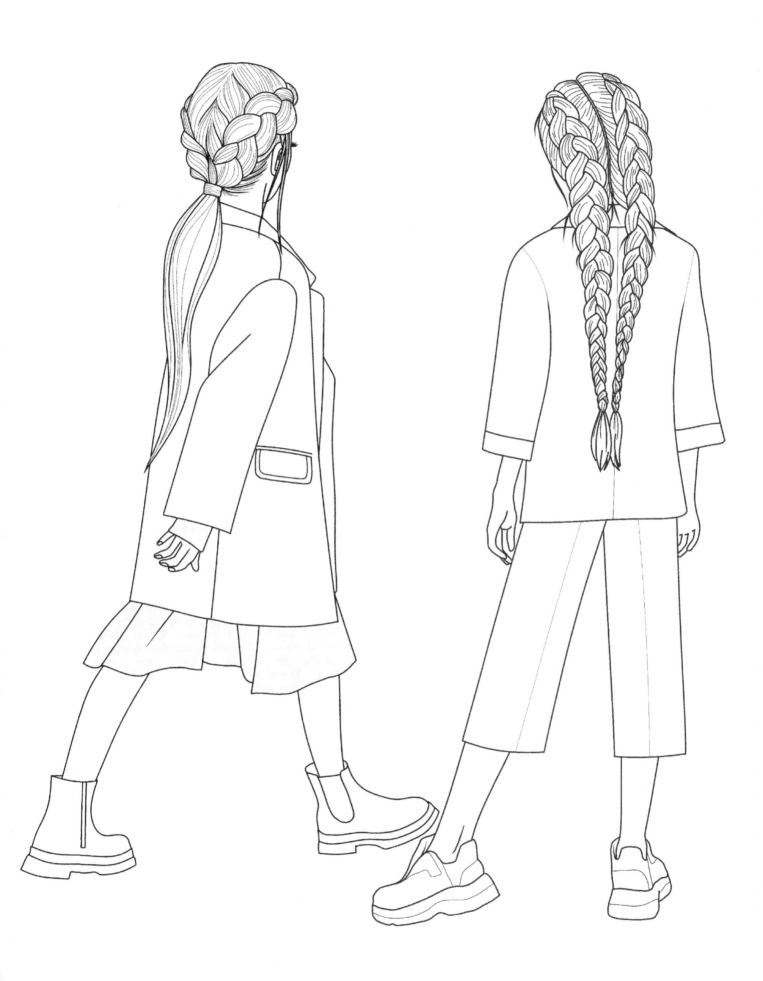

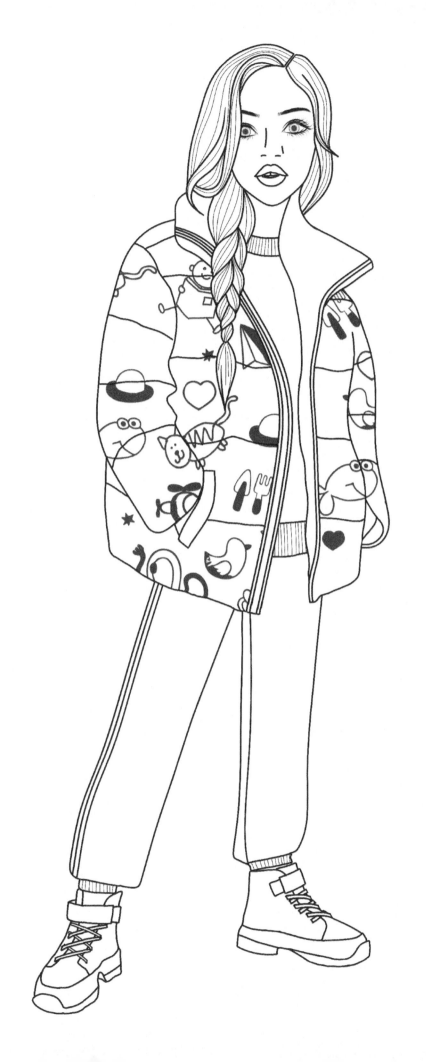

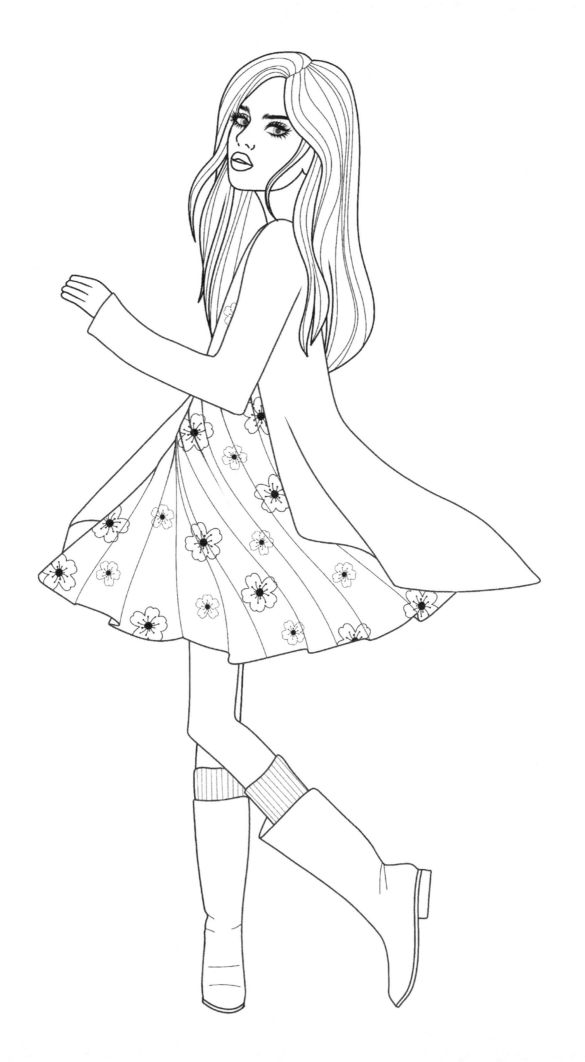

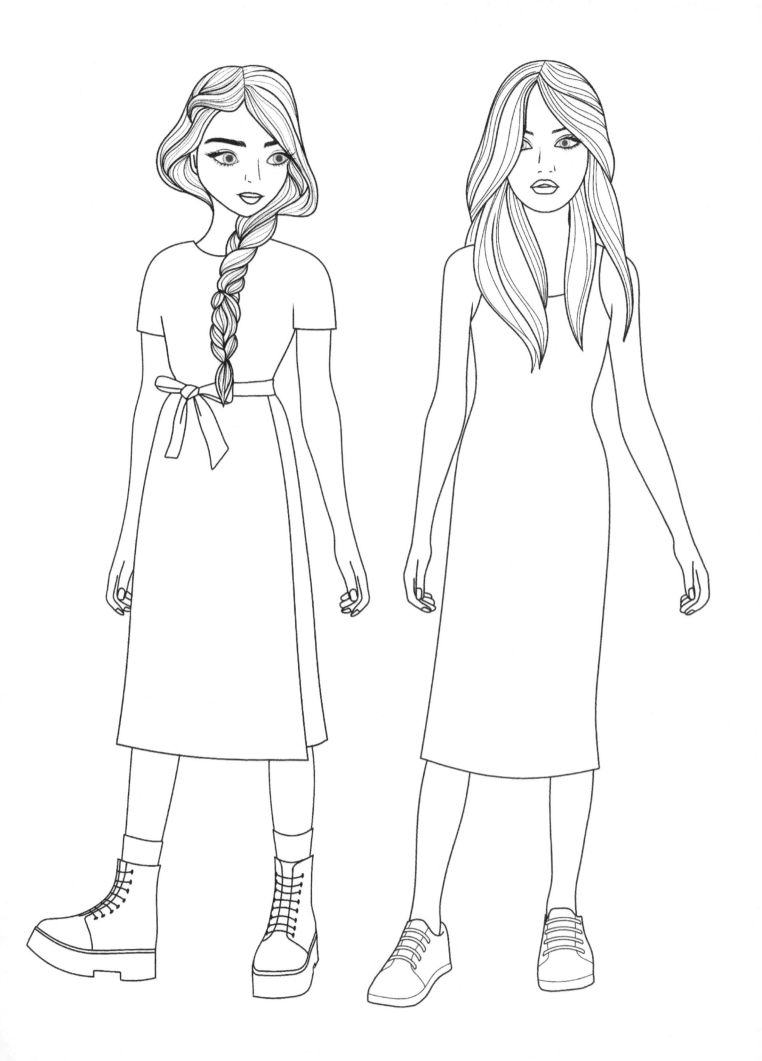

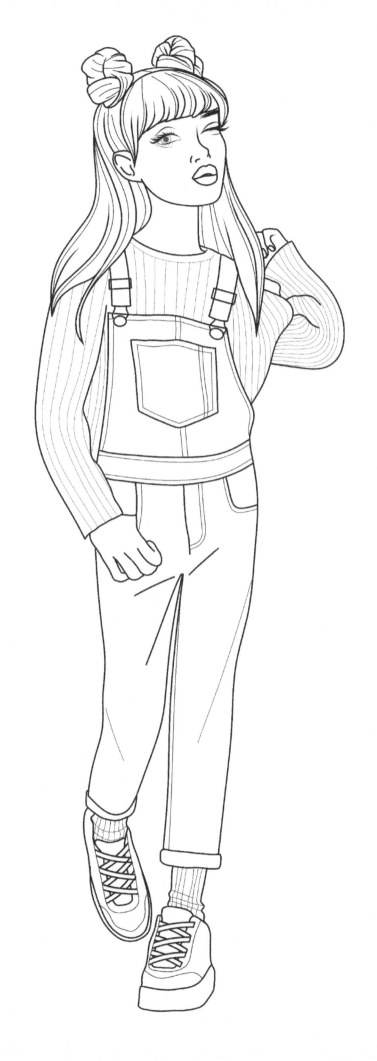

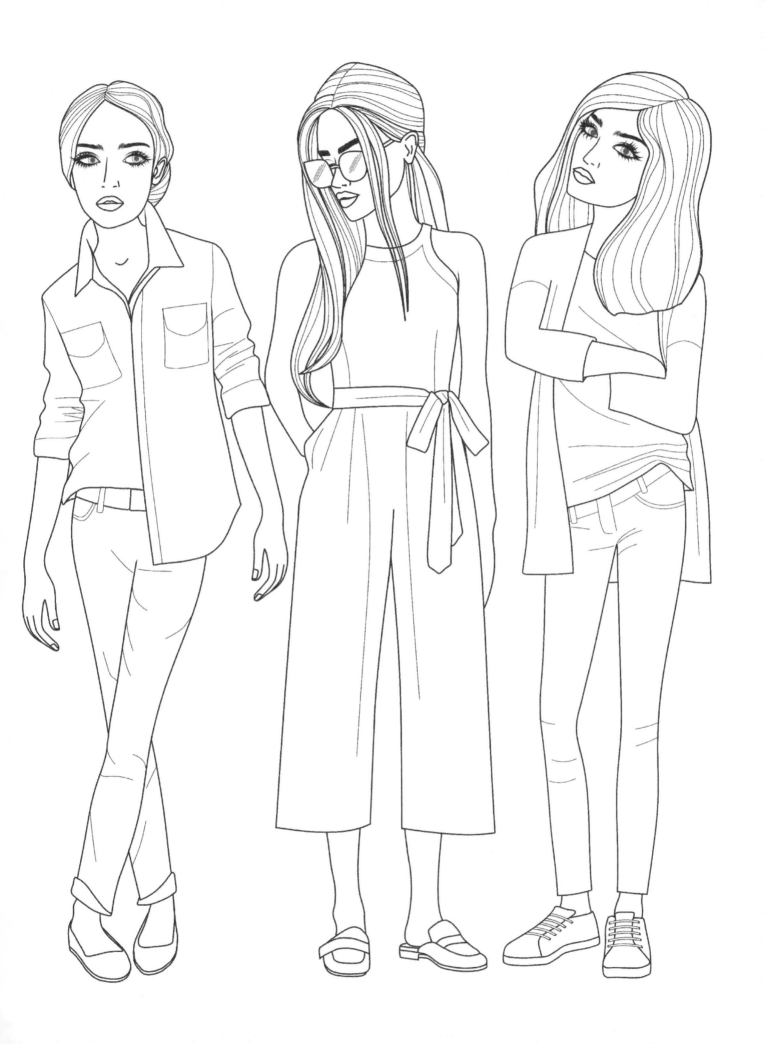

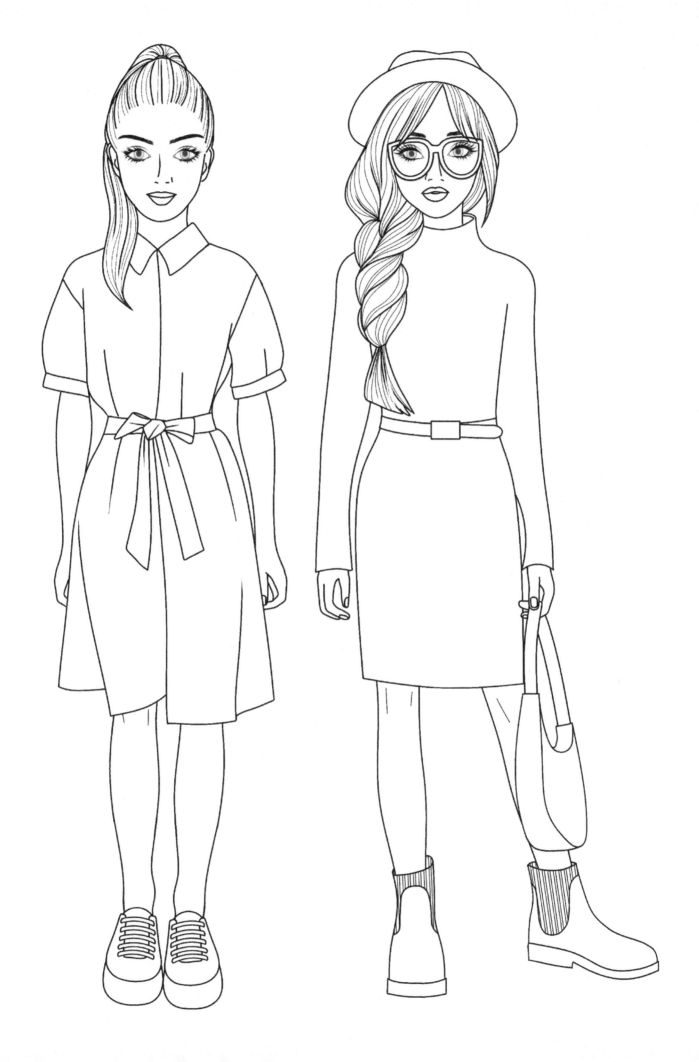

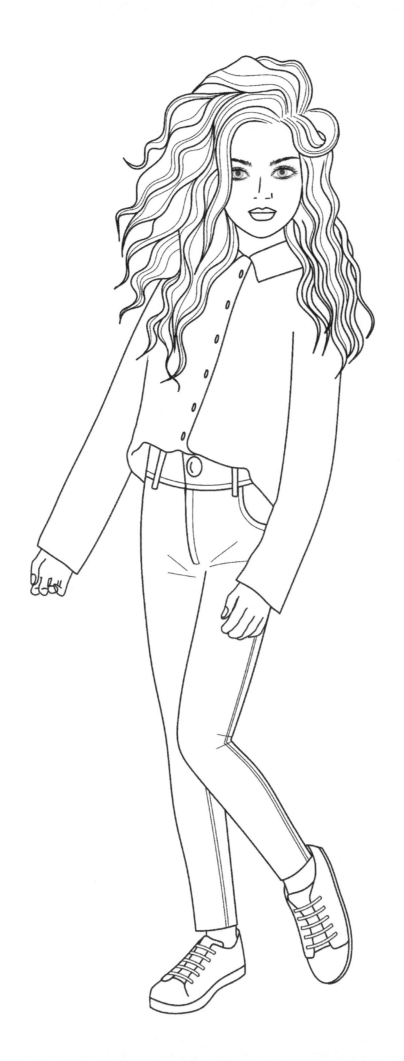

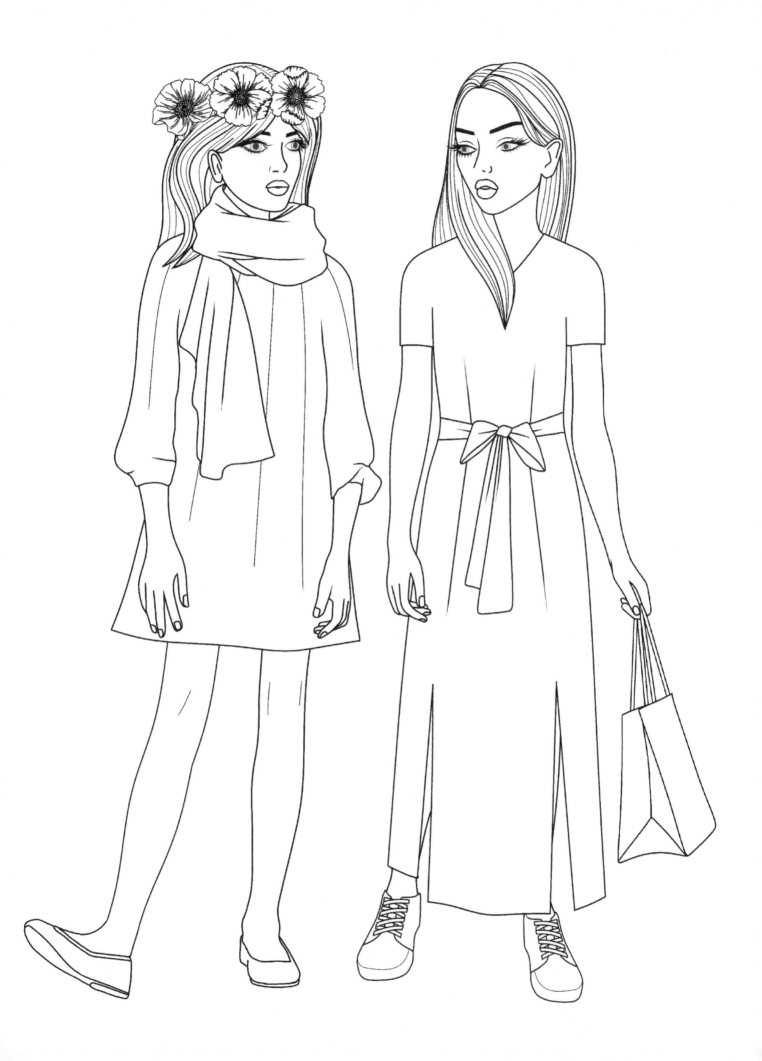

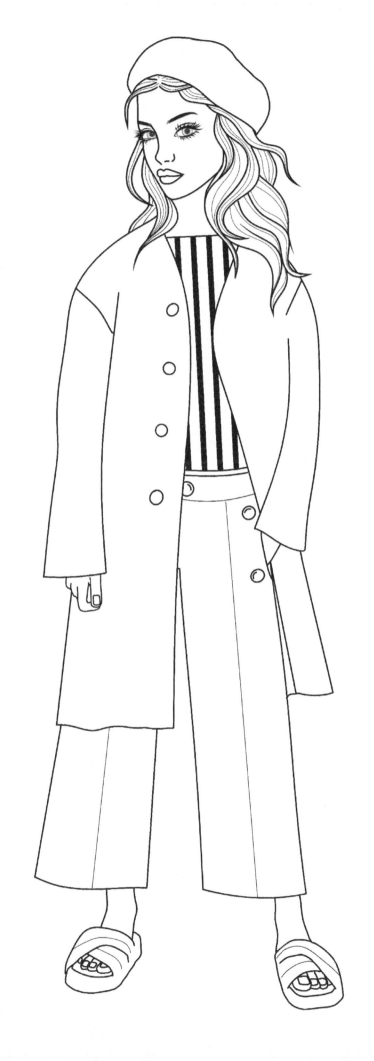

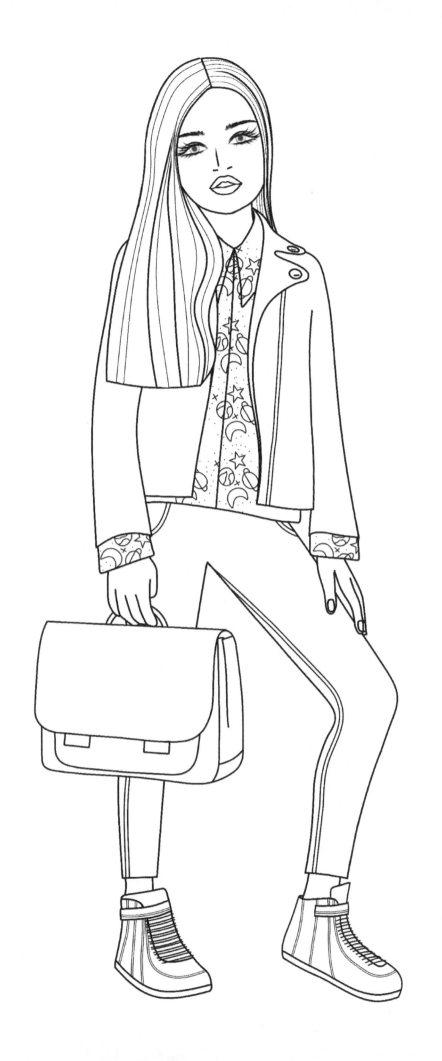

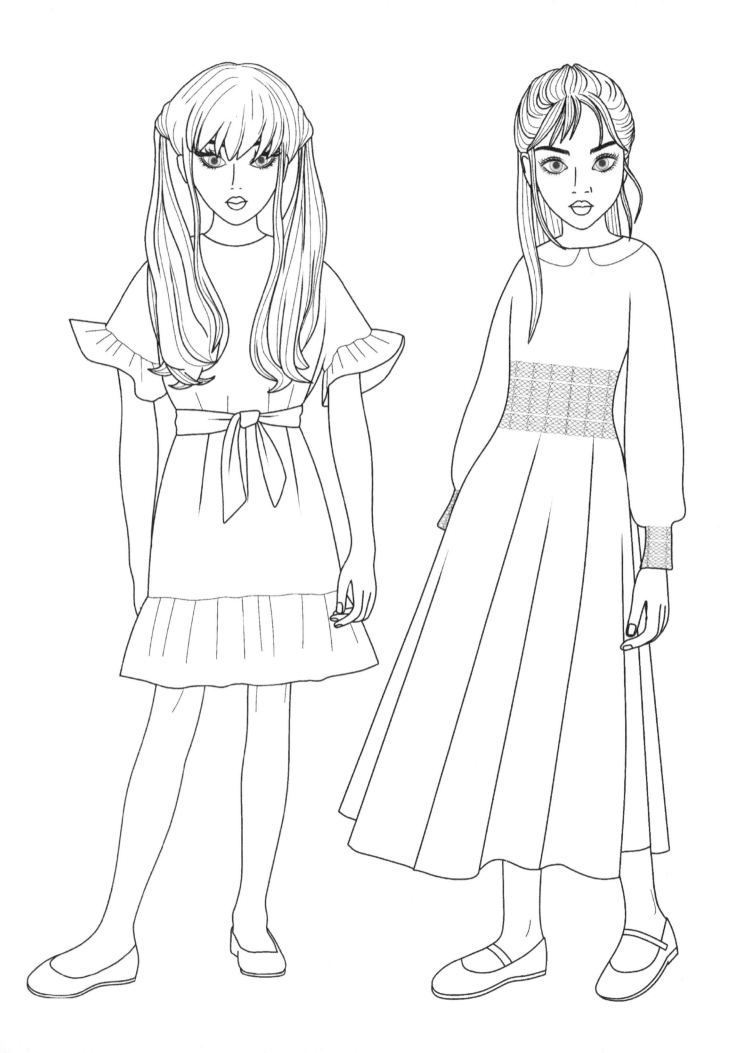

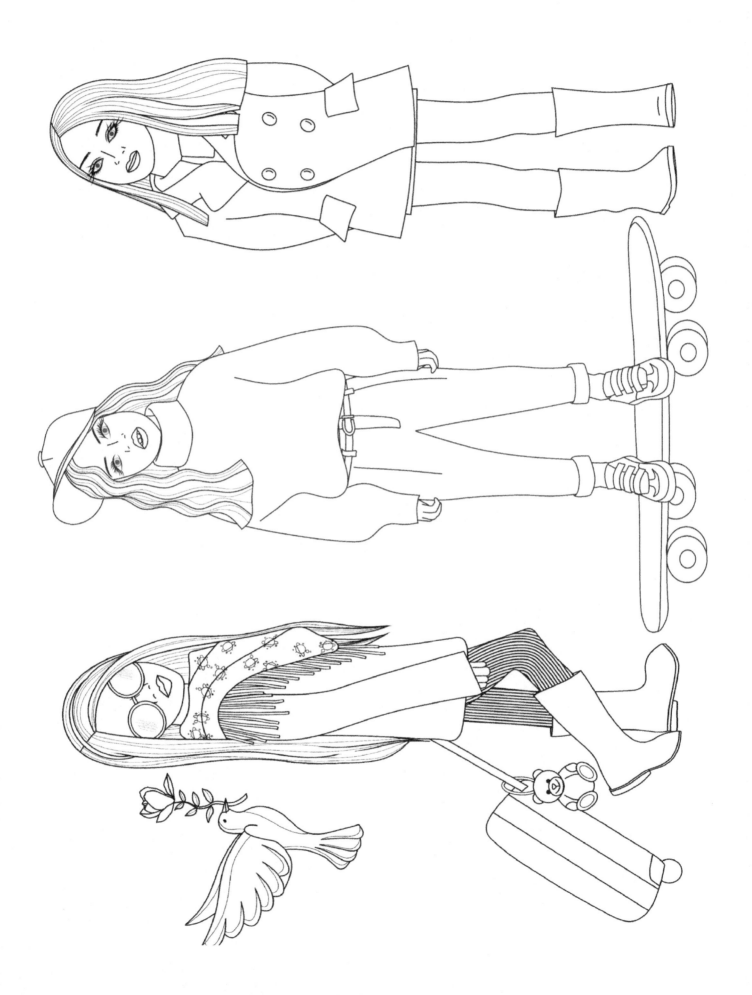

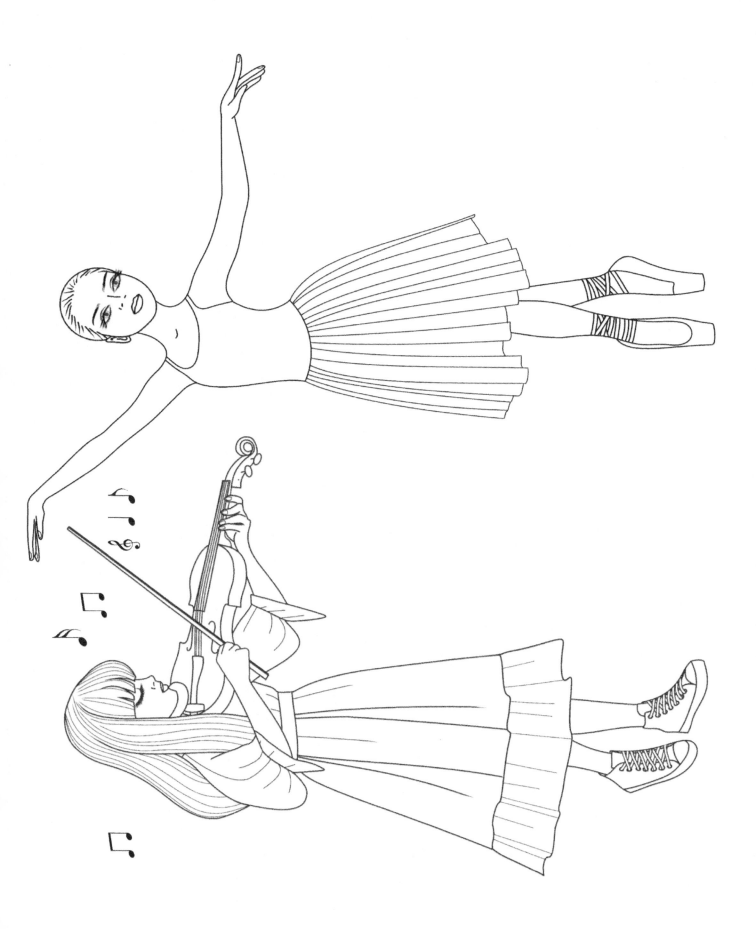

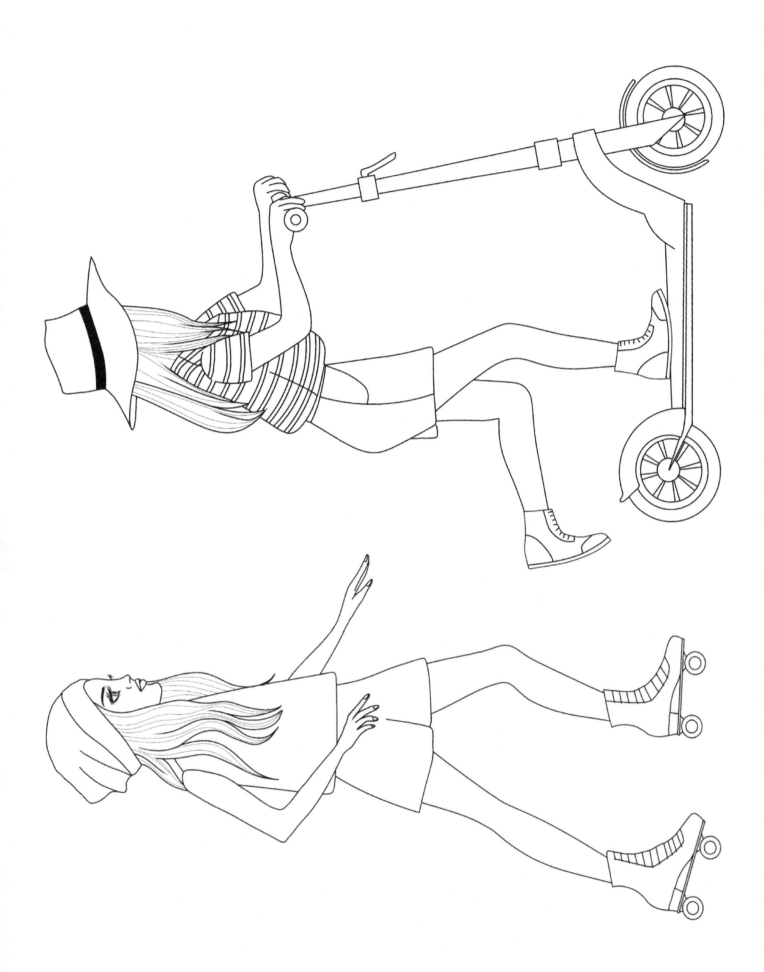

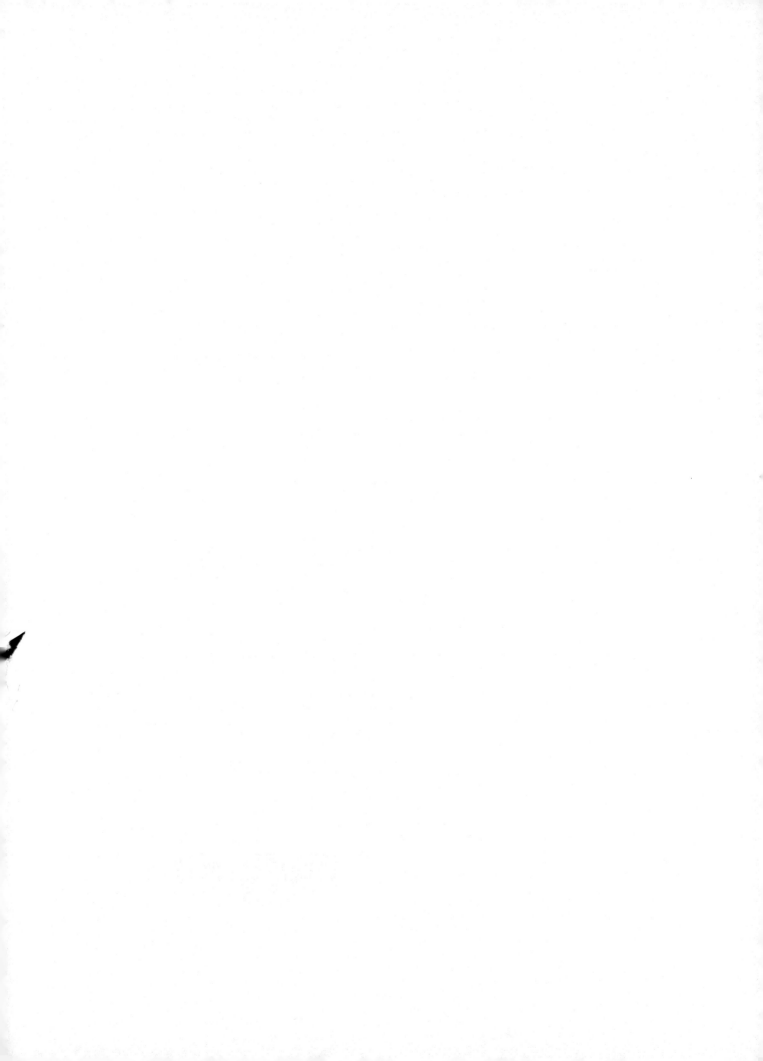

Made in the USA
Las Vegas, NV
03 March 2024

86641744R00063